Walter's War

and the Compassionate Heart

To Sylvia ~ a
dear and encouraging
friend ~
with love from
Helen :)

xx

Walter's War

and the Compassionate Heart

Helen O'Leary

DIADEM BOOKS

Walter's War and the Compassionate Heart
All Rights Reserved. Copyright © 2017 **Helen O'Leary**

No part of this book may be reproduced or transmitted in any form or by any means, graphic, electronic, or mechanical, including photocopying, recording, taping or by any information storage or retrieval system, without the permission in writing from the copyright holder.

The right of Helen O'Leary to be identified as the author of this work has been asserted in accordance with the Copyright, Designs and Patents Act 1988 sections 77 and 78.
Published by Diadem Books

For information, please contact:

Diadem Books
8 South Green Drive
Airth
Falkirk
FK2 8JP
Scotland UK
www.diadembooks.com

The views expressed in this work are solely those of the author and do not necessarily reflect the views of the publisher, and the publisher hereby disclaims any responsibility for them.

This work is about real people and the author has used sources in good faith and cannot be held responsible for inaccuracies.

ISBN: 978-0-244-34009-4

For Alice, Penny and Flora

Contents

Prologue		1
1.	The Thirteenth Child	3
2.	The Young Edwardians	25
3.	Just You Wait, Kaiser Bill	48
4.	A Near Miss	61
5.	Marking Time	85
6.	Passage to India	114
7.	Heat, Dust and Dysentery	124
8.	From Bombay to Burhan	151
9.	Hard Times	163
10.	Marching as to War	183
Gallery of Photographs		200
11.	In Alexander's Footsteps	210
12.	On Top of the World	227
13.	Turning Point	243
14.	Heaven's Gate	260
15.	Eighty Days in Baghdad	288

16.	Dogs of War and other Mercenaries	317
17.	Death of a General	332
18.	The Draughtsman's Desk	346
19.	Keep the Home Fires Burning	365
20.	Walter Finds his Feet	389

Epilogue	405
Six Poems and an Anecdote	415

Acknowledgements

Family, friends and colleagues

I'd never have written this book without Margaret and Andrew Barley who discovered Walter and Emma's correspondence in the linen bag.

My cousin Gill Alleeson, granddaughter of Percy, provided facts and photos from her comprehensive family archives and was tireless in replying to my endless questions.

Robina Lowry corrected several drafts as well as the final manuscript.

Jane Norrie, Susan Molbeck, Peter Brookes, Tracy Thomson of Sotogrande Writers, Alva Holland and other members of the Estepona Writing Group, gave positive criticism and encouragement.

Helena Buckland and Joan Speakman Wright helped check through the text at various stages.

Members of the Benahavis Decorative and Fine Arts Society invited me to read excerpts from the book at one of their lively quiz nights.

Simon Parker in Australia provided background information about the 1/25th Londons.

Anthony Gammie lent relevant literature and made well-informed and thought-provoking comments.

Monica Tross helped me to discover the wonders of the Imperial War Museum, London.

Susie Weir, Vanessa Hewlings and Nigel Killeen were among those who gave valuable criticism.

Pat and Lisa Mills were generous with publishing advice and contacts.

Natalie Gazdar enhanced old family photos.

* * *

The London Museum kindly granted permission to include John O'Connor's painting of the view of the St Pancras Hotel.

Sources

"Everything you want to know is on the Internet," says Gill Alleeson, a diligent and intuitive researcher. Wikipedia was very useful, but more traditional sources were the best of all, among them:

Chronicles of the 20th Century
1929 Encyclopedia Britannica
All Quiet on the Western Front, Erich Marie Remarque
Tommy's Ark, Richard Van Emden
The Fishing Fleet, Anne de Courcy
Plain Tales from the Raj, Charles Allen
The National Army Museum Book of the Turkish Front 1914-18, Field Marshall Lord Carver
The Beauty and the Sorrow, Peter Englund
When God Made Hell, Charles Townshend
The Fall of the Ottomans, Eugene Rogan
In the Shadow of the Sword, Tom Holland

Prologue

Letters in a linen bag

My mother used to pack our swimming things for the summer holidays in a battered cardboard suitcase with an expanding lid. It had belonged to my father before he was married.

Family holidays became a thing of the past. The suitcase was stuffed with papers, put in the attic and forgotten until, when my parents died, my brother and sister-in-law sorted through the family house and passed the suitcase on to me.

Inside was a linen bag. Just a bundle of letters, a few photos and old diaries. Then, as I transcribed the crumbling pages, I stepped back into the past and my father and his family came to life. Not as I knew them, the old aunties with bunions and hand-knitted woollies and Uncle Jim with his awful jokes and bad cough; they were young people whose subliminal images can still be traced in the faces and personalities of countless cousins and succeeding generations.

And there is my dad, their little brother, growing up and getting into scrapes before going off to War.

At the heart of Barley family life in the early 20th century was my grandmother, Emma, who through her letters is also at the heart of this story.

1

The Thirteenth Child

Walter stretched uncomfortably in the narrow bed he shared with his big brother Joe, forcing himself to switch from his pleasant dream to the cold reality of the January morning. He could hear the muffled plod of horses' hooves as laden buses passed the window, the ring of hobnailed boots on icy cobblestones and his mother calling out to the older children to get ready. There was a burst of chatter from the girls' room. Percy clattered down the stairs on his way to work and, from deep within the creaking bowels of the crowded old house, baby Horace started to howl.

He pulled the blanket from Joe's soundly sleeping body and snuggled into a narrow cocoon, waiting for his father to roar his usual reaction to Horace's howls. He mouthed the words he knew by heart:

'Get that child to pipe down or I'll give it a good hiding.'

He shut his eyes and let his imagination drift back into his dream of a land *'where the feathery palm-trees rise and the date grows ripe under sunny skies,'* a dream invoked by the poem his mother recited to him when he needed comforting.

Walter Ernest Barley, my father, was born on 22nd September 1895, the thirteenth child of Emma, née Povey, and James Barley, undertaker, of 97 Archibald Road, Kentish Town Road, St Pancras.

The Barleys and Poveys had lived side by side for several generations.

Diligent and hard-working, they were part of a close community of families and tradespeople who worked and worshipped together. They could turn their hands to producing whatever was in demand, becoming skilled craftsmen: builders, carpenters and, in a field where demand was constant, undertakers.

When she married, Emma was an upright, confident young woman of 23 with a level gaze and beautiful skin. Her bird-like brown eyes and dark hair were a legacy from a playboy French grandfather with a long name and a penchant for pretty women. Emma may well have worn a white wedding dress, a trend started by Queen Victoria, and the skirt would probably have had a bustle at the back, a fashionable way to enhance a tiny waist. It would also have helped to offset the noticeable bump in front which, five and a half months later, was to emerge as Auntie Lily.

The extravagant spires of St Pancras, rising above the smoke-choked streets of London in the 1880s, expressed the confidence and vitality of the Victorian era into which Walter was born. Although sunset skies were polluted, damp basements crawled with vermin, disease was rife and the rate of child mortality was high, things were looking up. You could hail a bus, post a letter, switch on a light and even flush a lavatory. Small boys were no longer pushed up chimneys and women were beginning to have a voice. An ageing Queen Victoria ruled not only the waves; she governed more of the world than anyone before or since.

The young Barleys were among the emerging upwardly-mobile working-class residents of London who had never had it so good.

This was the empire over which the sun never set.

The 1891 census describes James Barley as 'aged 40 years old and an undertaker (employer)'. They have a 16-year-old servant, Libby Harris. According to a contemporary survey of London streets, the inhabitants of the Kentish Town Road are, 'fairly comfortably off. Good ordinary earnings'.

James Barley was a tall, genial young man when he married Emma. A bit slack about the mouth, perhaps, but you could see why Emma was attracted to him. He was a talented cabinet-maker, although the opportunities for commercial success were limited in an area where houses were simply furnished and most items had been passed on by relatives. It was quite common at the time for carpenters to 'undertake' coffin-making and other duties for funeral directors and James was lucky; with Emma's hand in marriage came a flourishing funeral business and, according to a cousin, 'the finest team of horses in North London.'

Two more daughters, Gertie and Grace, were born in quick succession to Lily. Gertie flourished but Grace died in infancy. Although she would have been sadly mourned, the death of a child was a common occurrence and there were plenty of friends and family members who had lost small children of their own to share their grief. James would have presided at Grace's funeral as he had three years earlier at the interment of his sister's newly-born son, after whom he would name his own youngest child. The first Horace's memorial card reads:

> *In Loving Memory of*
> *Horace Cecil Hedges*
> *Who died January 16th 1883*
> *Aged 7 weeks. Interred at Finchley Cemetery.*
> *Released from Sorrow, Sin and Pain,*
> *And free from every care;*
> *By Angels' hands to Heaven conveyed,*
> *To rest for ever there.*

J. Barley, Undertaker, 97 Kentish Town Road.
(corner of Clarence Road), N.W.

The Barleys, like most Victorians, were not afraid of sentiment.

After six girls: Lily, Gertie, Grace, Daisy, Mabel and Violet, came Percival, Ethel, John (Jack), Ruby, James (Jim, James only to his mother) and Joseph (Joe), then Walter and finally Susan and Horace (Billie).

Finding space for all these offspring was a problem. Open any door and you'd find someone behind it: Susie having a knee bandaged, big sister Ruby sewing a fire-screen, Lily writing to her young man or Percy and Mabel playing cards or arguing over a musical score-sheet. Privacy was hard to come by. Even the semi-basement where Walter and Joe slept was stacked with bare wooden coffins ready for their final finish and eternal occupants. James liked to keep plenty in stock. Walter once spent so long lying in one during a game of hide-and-seek, he fell asleep. 'Woe betide you if I ever catch you being so disrespectful again,' James warned him. 'I could of been carried off in it,' replied Walter cheerfully. 'Have, not of,' retorted Ruby, overhearing.

Like the bunions the girls were to develop from their ill-fitting shoes, being right became a Barley family trait.

James was short tempered and regularly beat his children. But he was proud of his big family and spent time with them after work, playing cards with the older ones and romping with the toddlers. Victorian children expected physical chastisement and the effects of his occasional outbursts could be less hurtful than Emma's stern reprimands. As long as James's business flourished he was fun. An accomplished musician, he devoted some of his skills as a carpenter to making violins for Percy, Mabel and Horace, and a cello for Walter. This home-grown quartet performed with various degrees of skill and harmony with friends and at family parties.

Walter was a merry, bright little boy who adored his big brothers Percy and Jack, was bossed about by his older sisters and doted on by Violet. His name, like his clothes, was passed on from an older brother; James's second name was Walter.

He was eager to please but his enthusiasm sometimes ran away with him.

An enamelled bathtub stood in a small room half way up the stairs. For James's use only. No hot water was laid on – there was a cold tap in the kitchen. Jugs were heated on the cooking range and brought up in relays. Owning an enamelled bath was special, even though this one was chipped and rusty. A pot of shiny white paint and a brush had been left on the windowsill by Percy, who meant to 'give that old bath a lick of paint' in due course. Walter, ever helpful, had a go at it himself. It took him ages but he was pleased with the result. However, the paint dried very slowly and got sticky when hot water was poured on it. James, looking forward to relaxing after a long day's undertaking, was not pleased.

Emma oversaw a strict regime of personal hygiene, study and social skills. Nails must be clean, hair neatly brushed, hems straight. The children were taught 'Victorian values' – a sense of duty, responsibility and respect for older people and those in authority – but this was not a repressive family where children were seen and not heard.

Their lively arguments competed with the clanking of pre-plastic household implements, squawks from their father's cantankerous grey parrot and the frantic songs of the skylarks and canaries he kept caged in the back room where the children were not allowed.

This was where he would retreat in the evening with his papers and music when the birds and children were asleep. Walter, who had a weak chest, would sometimes be woken up by a fit of coughing. Lying in the dark, fighting to control it, he'd hear the sound of a violin. He would creep upstairs and find his sisters Ruby and Vi already outside the door, secretly listening to the sweet, sad tune James was playing to the sleeping parrot.

From dawn to dusk, the Barley household hummed. There were floors to be scrubbed, fires lit, clothes washed and darned, furniture waxed and windows washed. Once he was old enough, Walter gave a hand in the kitchen.

Carrie, a much-loved distant relative who for years had helped the Poveys and Barleys with child-minding and housekeeping, would tell him when to top up the huge stew-pots on the iron grate as the water bubbled away.

At Christmas he'd take his turn in mixing doughy cannonballs of plum puddings, tied up in muslin and steamed for hours. Condensation dripped down the windows. The silver threepenny pieces buried deep within the puddings were religiously returned by all the children except Billy. He hid his in his pocket. As far as he was concerned, good luck had to be implemented by hard cash.

Christmases were memorable. Ethel's daughter Irene recalled that 'there would be a Christmas tree and a piano and all who could perform. Everyone joined in the sing-songs and Grandma (Emma) would sit back looking happy and perfectly fulfilled with so many of her family around her. We would play endless games of cards and charades and there was always a box of farthings to be divided amongst the young ones and given as prizes. We would spend them on sweets at the earliest opportunity.'

The older children looked after the younger ones. Sister Lily taught Walter to read. Sister Vi ironed his collars and blacked his boots. Brother Jack listened to his stories and Jim protected him from the school bullies. Percy, a talented musician, tried to teach him the cello but Walter was not an enthusiastic pupil. When he should have been practising his scales, he would be daydreaming or asking questions no-one could answer.

Meals were taken together as a family. The children were always hungry and Walter soon learned that if he took his eyes off his plate when mischievous brother Jim said, 'Look Wallie, over there,' the tasty piece of mutton he had been saving for last would disappear. He ate everything, even the fat, down to the very last morsel. By the standards of the time their diet was reasonable, although lacking in leafy vegetables. Emma would boil down bones, adding bay leaves, nutmeg and cloves to flavour the broth for a soup which would last for days. Fresh fruit was a luxury. If they were lucky the children would occasionally get a segment of orange each. A weekly purge of castor oil kept them 'regular'.

Before James took his place at the head of the table Emma would warn the little ones to keep their voices down in case he was in a bad mood. Increasingly, though, he would roll home merry from a gathering of undertakers. Perhaps because of the need to relax after the solemn nature of their work, most of James's colleagues enjoyed socialising over a pint or two of ale.

A contemporary report declared that, 'contrary to the popular idea, undertakers, out of business hours, are particularly light-hearted as a class, and have a keen sense of humour.' A business is advertised as offering an 'excellent opening for energetic man willing to put his heart into the work'. Numbered among its attractions: 'Sanitary arrangements much neglected; mortality from fevers excessively high; total death-rate 10.7% higher than any town within radius of fifty miles; one trade competitor (carpenter) only.' Graveyard humour prevailed.

Funerary customs had relaxed considerably during Victoria's reign. Months of mourning were no longer observed; the days when mutes were hired to stand outside the grieving household had gone. Extravagant black veils and plumes were modified. Flowers, which in the 1850s were never seen, were placed on coffins by the bereaved. Some undertakers did not approve, complaining that all these floral tributes hid their fine work.

James Barley moved with the times; his carefully-carved coffins were no longer completely black but finished with a clear varnish and brass trimmings. His well-groomed horses and immaculate hearse carried his deceased neighbours on their last journey without the heavy formality of previous years.

It was sister Vi who told Walter that the Queen had died. She was getting him ready for school, helping to button his boots although he could do them by himself given half a chance.

Walter frowned at the news. Queen Victoria was very old. He knew what she looked like from the penny coin he had earned from running errands for old Mrs Henderson next door. The profile of the Queen showed her veil draped back from her coronet to her shoulder so you could see her double chin and pointed nose. He'd polished it until every bead on her necklace gleamed like a pinpoint of gold. Walter knew the wording round the rim by heart: 'VICTORIA DEI GRA BRITT REGINA FID DEF IND IMP'. This was Latin and meant, Walter knew, because Lily had told him, 'Victoria by the Grace of God, Queen of the British territories, Defender of the Faith, Empress of India'.

He would join in lustily whenever the National Anthem was played. He knew the colonies were close to the Queen's heart and Percy and Jack would often talk about them. He wondered whether, one day, they would travel to the ends of the earth and explore the far flung reaches of the British Empire.

'Who will be Queen now?' he asked. 'Who will be Def Ind Imp?'

'It won't be a Queen,' said Vi, her face red from bending over Walter's boots. 'It will be a King.'

Queen Victoria had died at Osborne House on the Isle of Wight at 6.30am on 22nd January 1901, after a series of small strokes. An air of solemnity settled over London. People wore black and spoke in hushed voices. Jim was not allowed to recite 'It was not the cough that carried 'er off, but the coffin they carried 'er off in'. Walter tried to get used to singing 'God Save our *King*' instead of 'Queen', and 'send *him* victorious' instead of '*her*'. How strange it sounded!

Prince Albert's death in 1861, and a bad fall down the stairs at Windsor Castle soon after, had turned the Queen into a virtual recluse. Grief removed her from the public eye in a way her would-be assassins never had. 'It is worth being shot at to see how much one is loved,' she had remarked after the first of several attempts on her life. The deaths of three more people close to her affected her profoundly: her daughter Princess Alice of Hesse succumbed to diphtheria on the anniversary of Albert's demise in 1878; her favourite prime minister, the dashing Benjamin Disraeli, died in 1881 and her fine-looking Scottish servant, John Brown, died in 1883 having looked after her devotedly for more than 20 years. His role was taken over by an elegant young Indian, Abdul Karim, who introduced curry into the Royal kitchens and taught the Queen how to speak Urdu. Both servants were on close terms with the lonely, widowed queen, who repaid their loyalty with maternal affection.

Sentimental and generous with gifts, she cherished her personal mementoes and rituals. Every morning during the 40 years since Albert's death she'd had fresh clothes laid out on his bed. When John Brown died, a flower was placed on his pillow every day. One December she gave Abdul Karim a Christmas tree.

After lying in state for ten days, the Queen's body was taken aboard the royal yacht *Alberta* to travel to Portsmouth and onwards to Victoria Station by train, where a black steam engine puffed gently to a halt alongside a platform decorated in purple and knee deep in dignitaries. Her small coffin, draped in white satin under her personal flag, was placed on a gun carriage drawn by eight white horses. On top were the Imperial State Crown, two orbs and a sceptre. Only a purple bow made any concession to funerary pomp. In silence, apart from the chink of sheathed swords and harnesses, the royal mourners took their places for the long, slow procession to Paddington Station.

Immediately behind the coffin rode the new King, Edward VII. The *Illustrated London News* reported that his 'familiar face was grave and seemed careworn. He looked straight ahead, seemingly at the gun carriage on which was the body of the sovereign whose glory and responsibilities he had inherited. He did not see, or gave no sign of seeing, the long ranks of soldiers hedging back the populace about him, the windows crowded with black bonneted women, the multitudes of uncovered heads, the purple draperies, and the green wreaths everywhere. He passed like a man alone.'

On the king's right rode his nephew Kaiser Wilhelm II, Emperor of Germany, the Queen's favourite grandson and at the time a popular public figure. He 'looked every inch a soldier and commander of men' as he acknowledged the recognition of the crowd. It is said that the Queen had died in the Kaiser's arms.

Many sayings attributed to the Queen, like 'We are not amused', don't stand up to scrutiny. We certainly know from her surviving letters that Victoria was nowhere as starchy as she is made out to be and was amused quite often. If she seldom broke into a broad smile it was probably because her teeth, like those of most of her generation, were not her best feature. Dentistry was primitive, even for the Queen.

Victoria had banned black for her personal entourage. Instead, scarlet uniforms and gold-encrusted carriages made a shimmering ribbon of colour as the funeral procession made its way to Paddington through the solemn crowd, in the thick of which were Percy and Walter.

Half the population of London must have been out there watching her last journey. There was barely space to stand and groups of onlookers climbed into the bare branches of the young London plane trees where they swayed like flocks of giant black vultures.

Percy hoisted Walter onto his thin shoulders. The little boy's nose ran in the cold and he pressed his face into the back of

Percy's cloth cap, making a damp patch on the scratchy woollen fabric. He could hear the subdued beat of a drum. Snatches of sombre music carried on the wind.

'Look Wally,' Percy whispered as the coffin came into view, 'Say goodbye to Her Majesty.'

A few tears rolled down Walter's pink cheeks and further dampened Percy's cap as he peered through the top hats and black bonnets of the crowd. He caught a glimpse of the tossing heads of the white horses and the coffin. Only a glimpse, but Walter was to remember it all his life.

Percy and Walter made their way home through the crowds which thinned out as they got nearer St Pancras. Percy hummed the tune of Beethoven's funeral march and Walter walked slowly and sturdily in time to it, his little arms working to and fro until he got tired. It was a long way and the day was still bitingly cold and windy. Torn patches of smoke from rows of chimney stacks were sucked up into the yellowish sky.

They reached the shelter of a side street of red-brick houses. The blinds at the tall windows closed as a mark of respect to the dead Queen. Walter picked up a stick and dragged it along the intricate cast-iron railings, making a wonderful syncopated sound. 'Please don't do that,' said Percy. He stopped, but only because it was Percy who had asked him.

Once at home in the warmth of the kitchen, Walter told his sisters what they'd seen: the crown on the coffin, with real diamonds, the bright red uniforms, lots of gold jingling on the horses...

'Not black? I'd thought everything would be black,' said Ruby, who would have dearly loved a pair of shiny jet earrings.

As the children of an undertaker, they knew something about funerals. The girls used to help their mother to pleat and hem the purple satin linings of the coffins brought up from the basement as they were needed.

In 1901 it 'was not done' to discuss sex, money or politics, but there were no such inhibitions about death. The girls knew that

Emma was involved in the sad task of dressing the bodies and that James was sometimes asked to place mementoes in the hands of the deceased. The children gossiped among themselves and were curious to know what had been placed in Victoria's coffin.

'She'd have worn her wedding veil and held a lock of Prince Albert's hair,' contended romantic Vi.

Jack wandered in. Walter offered him a piece of the bun Vi had buttered for him. 'More likely John Brown's,' said Ruby, 'Prince Albert was bald.' 'Wasn't Mr Brown prime minister?' asked Jack, who at twelve was not very well informed about politics. Vi and Ruby exchanged a glance and burst out laughing. Walter knew then and there that girls could be very silly indeed.

Rumours abounded although there were no tabloid newspaper reporters to scavenge among the skeletons in the Royal family's cupboards. Was the lock of hair the Queen held in her hand John Brown's, as Ruby wondered? Was she wearing his mother's wedding ring? Or was this just gossip?

The Scottish ghillie may have taken her cups of tea in bed and she was overheard calling him 'darling'. She called Benjamin Distraeli darling too, and sent him Valentine cards. That doesn't mean she was on more intimate terms with either of them. Victoria had a lonely job, and was still grieving over the death of her husband. Disappointed in her son and heir, she needed someone to turn to.

Edward destroyed all the correspondence between his mother and her two servants as soon as she died.

With the arrival of spring, the long Victorian epoch era rolled away into the past. New green leaves formed a haze over the plane trees and James's caged canaries and skylarks nearly sang themselves off their perches.

2

The young Edwardians

*You see things and say 'Why?'
But I dream things that never were and say
'Why not?'
(George Bernard Shaw)*

The boys continued to play spooky games in the basement, frightening their sister Ethel and her young man, Arthur Towner, when she took him down the dark stairway for a bit of peace and quiet.

His ardour was getting the better of his nervousness at the sight of the coffins until shapeless white figures arose from them, wailing and groaning, then collapsed into giggles as the boys pulled the sheets from over their heads. The young couple were not amused by their antics. Some years later earnest Ethel and ardent Arthur sailed with their three small children to Australia, as far as you could get from mischievous young brothers dressing up as ghosts, where they lived happily ever after.

Back in London, Walter and his siblings were growing up as young Edwardians. The new king was 59 when he came to the throne and reigned for barely ten years, but the Edwardian era – an age to be remembered for fashion and frivolity as much as reform and revolution – outlived him, lasting until the outbreak of World War One.

Edward soon emerged from the cloud he had lived under before his mother's death. A natty dresser, he loved hunting, racing and fun. He frequently strayed from his marital bed and his energy did not diminish with age and a broadening waistline. Victoria had regarded her son and heir as an irresponsible gadabout and blamed him for her beloved husband's death.

Albert was already ill when he heard of the student prince's escapade with a young actress. A stern reprimand was called for and he insisted upon travelling to Cambridge to deliver it in person. The journey made him worse and he died soon after. Queen Victoria told his sister Vicky that the sight of him made her shudder.

The British were looking forward to a lighter-hearted regime. The new monarch encouraged the arts, sport and the theatre. He took a great interest in food as well as fashion and introduced roast beef, Yorkshire pudding and horseradish sauce to the British Sunday lunch.

What 'Edward the Caresser' did in private was the subject of lively conjecture by Emma's knitting group, but she regarded his shenanigans as nobody's business but his own.

Where the widowed Victoria was aloof, Edward was outgoing, travelling around the country, meeting local dignitaries and treating ordinary people with charm and courtesy. He presided at the 1908 Olympic Games when Britain won 36 gold medals and national pride was at its peak. The public rejoiced in the new monarch's participation in public life.

He became the people's king.

There was a serious side to Edward's nature; he was concerned about the welfare of his subjects, many of whom endured excessively long working hours and terrible conditions in the new factories. For the impoverished young, childhood ended when they left school, often when they were only 12 years old. For those who had only ever known life in the workhouse, it never really began.

During his reign various social reforms were introduced, including subsidised secondary education in 1902 and old-age pensions in 1908. The groundwork was laid for national health insurance in 1909 but plans to fund it from a tax on landowners caused a budgetary crisis. When Prime Minister Asquith suggested to Edward that he should create new peerages to swing the vote in order to overthrow it, he refused. The act was passed by the Liberal government a year later.

In spite of the prosperity brought about by industrialisation and overseas trade, these were turbulent times as the rich got richer and the poor stayed where they were. As well as strikes and demonstrations at home there were tensions abroad as old regimes crumbled and new ones strove to take their place. Edward, related to most of the crowned heads in Europe, worked hard to keep the peace. However, the warlike behaviour of Kaiser Wilhelm II and the growth of his navy had become a thorn in his flesh. The Kaiser was surprised to find his English uncle's disapproval was shared by the British public. Had he not always been their friend? Germany had earned 'her place in the sun' and she needed strong defences to protect it. He would never understand why the British, with the biggest navy in the world, had not allied herself with Germany, with the biggest army. However, if they were against him, they should not blame the Germans for developing a large and powerful navy of their own.

The *Daily Mail* warned in an article in 1909: 'Britain alone stands in the way of Germany's path to world power and domination.' The end of his reign was a particularly troubling time for the King, who was often petulant with his ministers and tetchy at home. Alice Keppel, the most wise and steadfast of his many mistresses, was always ready to soothe his troubled brow.

To most of its inhabitants, Edwardian England still felt like the safest place you could be. Invincible, in spite of the posturing of the Kaiser.

Politics did not interest the Barley girls but fashion and the Royal Family did. They pored over black-and-white photos of the King and Queen at receptions and races, secretly scanning the pages for the pictures of the witty, bridge-playing Mrs Keppel. They got rid of their corsets, deepened their décolletages and trimmed the biggest hats they could afford with feathers and flowers.

They loved weddings. Discussions of wedding gowns, linens and honeymoons took place and trousseau boxes were prepared long before any of them went to the altar. Gertie had been the first to marry, in 1899 when she was nineteen. By 1904 a whole bunch of nuptials was in the offing. There was a flurry of excitement when Lily became engaged to Alan Brodie. Lily would spend hours getting ready for him to take her out, waiting for his special whistle as he strolled down the road to collect her.

The moment she heard it she'd rush downstairs, cheeks pink, hairpins flying, her long skirt bunched up in her hand, only to find James's beloved parrot, on its own, nonchalantly studying its toenails. It was a perfect mimic.

Nevertheless plans for the November wedding progressed smoothly and all went well on the day.

The following announcement appeared in the local newspaper:

WEDDING Brodie-Barley

A pretty wedding took place on Wednesday at Holy Trinity Church, Clarence road, the contracting parties being Mr Colin Alan Brodie, eldest son of Mr C.A. Brodie, of Burghley road, and Lillian Susie, eldest daughter of Mr James Barley, of 97 Kentish Town road. The bride, who wore cream crepe de chine, was attended by the Misses Mabel and Daisy Barley, sisters, while two younger children acted as train bearers. The bridegroom was supported by Mr W.A. James as groomsman, and the service was fully musical, with the organ being under the supervision of Mr Merry, of the Gospel Oak Congregational Church. The presents, which were very serviceable and costly, numbered over sixty, and were much admired by a numerous company of friends and relatives afterwards at the reception at 97, Kentish Town road. The happy couple later left for their honeymoon, which is to be spent in Surrey.

Three more weddings followed in quick succession: Ethel married Arthur, and Mabel her first husband, who wasn't considered good enough for high-flying Mabel. She divorced him soon after the birth of their daughter, Marjorie, and he was never again mentioned in the family. The third bride was Daisy. She married Bert Handley, who for years had peered through the fence to see what the Barleys were up to. Mabel used to describe him as 'the dirty urchin from next door' until he smartened himself up and was invited round to tea. Romance with Daisy blossomed and they were married in July 1905.

Emma and James hardly had time to breathe, let alone scrape up enough money for the dowries expected from Edwardian parents.

By now Walter could read fluently and knew several poems off by heart and would quote *The Boy Stood on the Burning Deck* to anyone who would listen. At the age of ten he was still fascinated by the scary fairy stories of Hans Christian Andersen. He told Joe about the witch's dog with eyes as big as saucers. Joe was unmoved. Impossible, he said. 'Not if it came very *very* near you,' said Walter, pushing his face into Joe's. Anything could happen in a fairy story. He tried to draw the dog (he was good at drawing) but it didn't work. There was another dog in the tale he didn't tell Joe about. This one had eyes as big as millstones. Walter realised that there are some things beyond anyone's imagination.

As he became too grown-up for fairy tales he continued to read avidly, borrowing well-thumbed adventure stories from his brothers. *Robinson Crusoe* and *Treasure Island* were his favourites. At weekends and on bank holidays, he and Joe would go to the British Museum and gaze at ancient inscriptions on fragments of stone and the great carved horses' heads from the Parthenon in Athens. What Walter enjoyed most were visits to the Natural History Museum with stuffed giraffes as tall as London's plane trees and a huge pit containing the great white bones of a whale.

He did well at school, thanks partly to encouragement at home but mostly due to his insatiable curiosity.

His drawings made him popular among his school fellows and he would pass cartoons of his teachers around the class. When 'Barley W' was hauled up to have his ears soundly boxed, 'Barley J' would feel rather proud of his younger brother's notoriety.

If Walter wasn't allowed to doodle, he'd daydream. Long church sermons provided a good setting for an imaginary adventure. The sermons at the nearby Free Christian Church suddenly became even more interesting than daydreams when Walter was about twelve. The new Unitarian Minister, the Reverend Fred Hankinson, was on the side of the liberal reformers of his day. His sermons were thought-provoking – full of ideas about achievement, hope and the importance of fighting for a fair society with better conditions for women and children.

The Barleys became enthusiastic members of Mr Hankinson's congregation and would stay behind after the Sunday service to talk to this small, dedicated man with kindly blue eyes. His new Sunday-school curriculum widened the younger Barleys' knowledge of literature and poetry and, through connections with influential benefactors, he organised visits to the countryside. He became a lifelong friend of the family and was always happy to discuss the ever-larger number of things Walter found beyond anyone's imagination.

Queen Victoria had already opened the doors to more liberal religious views by pushing through the Public Worship Bill in 1874. 'No more bowings and scrapings,' she had said.

To James and Emma, the Unitarians' humanist view of Christianity was an appealing reaction against the rigidity of the Anglican church. Unitarians believed in God as one person, rather than the trinity of three persons coexisting as one being. They could accept this but found the view of Jesus as a great man and a prophet of God, perhaps even a supernatural being, but not God himself, harder to accept.

Even if they did not always agree with the little minister, his sermons gave them a lot to talk and think about. Going to church on Sunday became an enjoyable social occasion as well as a duty.

Walter sang in the choir and his high treble voice rang out joyously as his mother and sisters, dressed in their Sunday best, took their seats among their friends and neighbours. He wondered whether Mr Hankinson might say something controversial; he had once been arrested for taking forbidden literature to the suffragettes he visited in prison. Undaunted, he went on preaching about women's rights.

Suffragettes had been actively campaigning for votes for women since the 1870s but, at about the time Mr Hankinson joined the Clarence Road church, they began to take more militant action. They chained themselves to railings, vandalised post boxes and set fire to the houses of politicians who opposed them. The Barleys were shocked. They had brought up their children to abide by the law. Would Mr Hankinson encourage them to rebel? They need not have worried. Apart from Mabel, they all agreed with their father that a woman's place was in the home.

Ironically, as James subsided into alcoholism, he spent more time at home than Emma and his daughters, retreating to his back room to play the violin or sitting morosely by the fire over his newspaper. He neglected his business and with six young children still to support the 'good ordinary earnings' were stretched so far that now it was hard to make ends meet.

Walter was often at home too, told to take a few days off school with 'one of his chests'. He would sit by the fire with his father, trying to cheer him up with his stories and his drawings until he was put to bed, his chest wrapped round with brown paper spread with mustard. A bout of ill health caused him to miss the opportunity of being selected for entry to the Bluecoat School and the chance of a scholarship and a good, classical education.

This was a big disappointment in his young life; the downturn in the family fortunes meant there was no money to pay for more than a basic education for the younger children and Walter left school at 14.

'It doesn't matter what happens to a man, but it does matter how he takes it. That's the true spirit of an Edwardian gentleman,' said Edward Marsh, a friend of fashionable architect Edwin Lutyens and an advocate of the stiff upper lip.

At first Walter accepted his fate stoically. He found a job at the nearby Express Dairy depot, helping to back the horses into their carts and load up the heavy milk churns. He loved working with the big, patient animals. But at the back of his mind he yearned for 'the better land'. It was, he felt, a very long way beyond his reach.

With his lack of formal education, Walter feared he might always be stuck in a job with no prospects. He could see with his own eyes the enormous contrasts between rich and poor.

He, his family and many of their friends were on the wrong side of the Great Divide between the classes. It would be a struggle to improve his own conditions, even if he studied in his spare time and worked hard.

But what about the others? The unemployed, the really poor and downtrodden?

'Times will change,' said Mr Hankinson.

More passionate, powerful people than Walter were speaking out against inequality. One of the great liberal orators of the day, Lloyd George, had expressed the sense of injustice felt by the working population at a rally in Newcastle in 1909:

'Who made ten thousand people owners of the soil, and the rest of us trespassers in the land of our birth?'

Winston Churchill, the Liberal government's President of the Board of Trade, was beginning to flex his own oratorical muscles as he warned that the country was at the crossroads: 'If we stand on in the old happy-go-lucky way, the richer classes ever growing in wealth and in number, and ever declining responsibility, the very poor remaining plunged or plunging even deeper into helpless, hopeless misery, then I think there is nothing before us but savage strife between class and class.'

Anarchy was in the air. Lenin came to London and on several occasions visited the British Museum's library (forerunner of today's British Library), describing it as an 'excellent institution, especially that exceptional reference system'.

Left-wing intellectuals who had been forming little pockets of dissension since the end of Victoria's reign began to have an influence. Two young Rossetti sisters, nieces of poet Christina, painter Dante Gabriel and daughters of a founding member of the Pre-Raphaelites, published an anarchist journal, *The Torch,* and became the nucleus of a prominent salon for dissident writers, artists and reformers. Playwright George Bernard Shaw wrote a pamphlet for them called *Why I am an Anarchist.*

A more moderate political campaigner than some of his writings suggested, Shaw was a prominent member of the Fabian Society, the small but highly influential left-wing movement which campaigned for a minimum wage, national health and education systems, the abolition of hereditary peerages and the nationalisation of land. It appealed mostly to middle-class intellectuals, including Fred Hankinson's sister Mary, but whilst it never attracted a large number of members, nearly all the early socialists and trade union leaders belonged to it. Fabianism! Walter liked the sound of it but he was too far below the parapet in years and social standing to be involved.

One day, decades later, when he had climbed a little way up the parapet, he piled my mother, little brother and me into the back of the old Austin A40, with Mr Hankinson in the front seat, and drove us out to a village green in the Chilterns to look at a park bench dedicated to Mary.

An outspoken suffragette and a friend of George Bernard Shaw, Mary Hankinson was a prominent Fabian, organising summer schools for the young, captaining their cricket teams, drilling their country dances and policing their morals. She was a bossy battleaxe, but she was also sharp-witted, charismatic and a natural leader. She taught Shaw to waltz backwards – 'he so tall and thin, she so short and square-shaped,' said the *Manchester Guardian*. When his play, *St Joan*, was published, he presented her with a copy inscribed: 'To Mary Hankinson, the only woman I know who does not believe she was the model for St Joan, and also the only woman who actually was.' Although he told several society women and famous actresses the same thing, there was probably a grain of truth in what he wrote.

In any case, it's good to think Mary left more than a park bench to posterity.

Not only was Shaw his sister's occasional dancing partner, he was a Borough Councillor in St Pancras, and instigated plans for the first ladies' public lavatory in nearby Camden Town. This may seem trivial when inmates of the local workhouse still lived in horribly overcrowded conditions and picked oakum – pulling apart lengths of filthy old rope to recycle as caulking for ships and water pipes – but even this small gesture made a tangible contribution to the emancipation of local women. It was a subject of conversation between Emma and her friends even though they would never have used it. Powdering one's nose in public? Someone might have overheard!

Walter was sixteen when the family left the Kentish Town Road.

By then Percy, 25, was a Life Insurance Agent. James, 21, was in the tobacco trade. Joe was 17 and an ironmonger's assistant. Jack had sailed for the Antipodes. Ruby was 'a lady clerk'. Walter was taking a while to settle into a proper job. Susie and Horace were still at school. The older children did not earn enough to support the rest of the family, so it was decided to rent somewhere smaller. For a while they lived at 21 Leighton Crescent before moving to 27 Archibald Road, a four-storey terraced house where James and Emma were to spend most of the rest of their lives and which stayed in the family until the nineteen-forties.

Walter felt constrained amid the noisy tumble of life in the new Barley home until he acquired a bicycle, thanks to some money from Mabel as a consolation present for missing the opportunity of winning a scholarship to the Bluecoat School. This revolutionised his life.

While the rich were beginning to take to the road in fantastic motor cars by Daimler, Lagonda or Rolls-Royce, this inexpensive Victorian invention was opening new avenues for young men like Walter. The 'safety bicycle', with two low wheels driven by a chain and pedals, instead of a higher wheel at the front with pedals fixed to its hub, came into its own in the nineteen-hundreds.

People of ordinary means could now work further away from home, explore the countryside in their leisure time and discover the freedom of travelling to places beyond walking distance from where they lived. Women were quick to discover the joys of cycling. The cross-bar was lowered to allow for more dignified mounting than cocking one leg over the saddle. Chain guards protected skirts from oil and small holes in the sides of back mudguards had threads drawn through them to stop long skirts from catching in the spokes of the wheel.

Walter pedalled energetically through open fields to Harrow, visiting sister Lily and Alan in their small terraced house, and on through the villages of Pinner and Rickmansworth to the foothills of the Chilterns where Mabel would give him a warm welcome in her pretty country cottage. He cycled along quiet Kentish lanes, ventured into the Surrey hills and went camping in farmers' fields, watching the stars by night and listening to the steady munching of an old horse which kept him company and occasionally nibbled gently at his boots.

All this open air and exercise helped Walter to grow into a strong, healthy young man. Not too tall, a bit short in the leg, he had a straight back, fair hair and an attractive smile. He'd greet fellow cyclists like old friends and pause to watch the occasional passing car. He'd wave at the driver who would give him a friendly hoot. It had been many generations since the Barleys were farmers in East Anglia, but the countryside was in Walter's blood. He took pleasure in propping his bike against a gate on hot summer days, chewing the end of a piece of grass as the farm-hands deftly arranged bundles of straw into corn-stooks. He'd give them a hand in return for a night's rest in a barn and a mug full of fresh milk in the morning.

Occasionally he ventured up a long, leafy lane to a country house where, as often as not, a nice lady with a big hat and gardening gloves would invite him in for a cup of tea in her drawing room. Such was Walter's charm and the classless appeal of his means of transport.

He often took a sketchbook on his travels and his drawing became good enough to get him a job in a draughtsman's office in London. It was pretty routine stuff, tracing, copying, lettering, learning how to use the protractors and instruments of the trade. But he was good at it and sufficiently well-paid to buy new clothes rather than wearing cast-offs, take up smoking and enjoy occasional visits to the theatre and recitals at concert-halls.

On the summer bank holiday of August 1914, Walter was in Herne Bay with Jim and Ruby,

Jim's girlfriend Dorrie and Ruby's fiancé, their first cousin, Joe Povey. It would have seemed like any normal sunny day at the seaside. They took the little tram along the pier, laughed at the 'What the Butler Saw' machines in the Pavilion and strolled along the promenade above serried ranks of wooden breakwaters. The wind ruffled Dorrie's dark, neatly-crimped waves. Jim told her she was beautiful. Ruby, famous for not speaking to people, most probably had her back to the group, shielding herself from the wind with her stiff black umbrella, her long skirt tugging at her ankles. As for Joe Povey, well, nobody ever knew with Joe Povey. And Walter? He was probably teasing Ruby when they heard that war had broken out.

Three years later, lying in a hospital bed in Baghdad, Walter recalled that day in his diary:

Ah, what a time! I cycled home via Gravesend, Chatham, Woolwich & arriving at Whitehall threaded through huge crowds waiting for news from Downing Street. How little we thought of the great crisis impending and the price – three years & millions of men gone across the borderland whilst others still fall.

3

Just you wait, Kaiser Bill!

Owing to the summary rejection by the German Government of the request made by his Majesty's Government for assurances that the neutrality of Belgium will be respected, his Majesty's Ambassador to Berlin has received his passport, and his Majesty's Government declared to the German Government that a state of war exists between Great Britain and Germany as from 11 p.m. on August 4, 1914.
(Foreign Office announcement.)

London buzzed with excitement at the news. People gathered in the streets and neighbours who hadn't spoken for ages got into animated conversation. 'Just you wait, Kaiser Bill,' they said. He'd get what was coming to him, they said. 'And, mark my words, it will all be over by Christmas.' A huge crowd gathered at Buckingham Palace to demonstrate overwhelming support for King George V and Queen Mary. There was a feeling of togetherness the country had not known for years.

Walter was swept up in the prevailing mood of patriotism and elation. Still only 18, his view of war was boyishly romantic – knights in shining armour from the stories he'd read, upright young officers quelling rebellions in the colonies, girls swooning at his feet as he marched past them in his uniform. But this was real. He could feel the blood coursing faster in his veins at the thought. He'd fight for his king and country. He'd die to protect his family and loved ones. He'd be like that boy in the poem who stood on the burning deck 'whence all but he had fled'.

Only sometimes, in the quiet hours before morning, he wondered what it would be like to come face to face with an enemy soldier. He asked Jim, already a member of the Territorial Army's Special Reserve. He knew about such things. 'You stick 'im in the ribs,' said his kindly brother, 'until 'e's dead.' He knew Jim was joking, or he hoped he was.

Within weeks, British troops suffered their first defeat, at Mons, not far from Waterloo in Belgium. More than 1600 soldiers of the elite British Expeditionary Force were wiped out by German gunners pushing their way towards France. Wellington would have turned in his grave.

The army could not afford to continue losing its highly-trained soldiers at this rate and now looked to its reserves. Jim was sent almost immediately to France – the family bade him a tearful goodbye as he ruffled Dorrie's curls and ruined her pretty hairdo. 'I'll wait for you,' she promised. Walter was half-envious of the attention lavished on his older brother, looking so brave and proud in his uniform.

The retreat from Mons only encouraged public outrage against the Germans, and Walter forgot all his doubts about fighting as soon as volunteers were needed. His country now needed *him!* He and Joe lost no time in joining the long queue of men and boys eager to enlist as they slowly wound their way towards the recruiting office. You had to be between 17 and 30 years old and taller than five feet three inches and fit, to be accepted. 'You'll come up to scratch,' said the older man behind them, but what about the little lad waiting in front of them? How old was he? 'Lumme, I dunno,' said the boy. 'Well, you better be seventeen by the time you get to the 'ead of the queue,' came the reply.

No documents were needed. You just gave your name, address and next of kin and a few personal details, underwent a brief physical examination and that was it. Public school boys on one side to be groomed as officers, the rest sent home to await a travel warrant and detailed instructions. The recruiting officer looked surprised when well-spoken young Walter said no, he hadn't been to a public school, actually.

Early volunteers were allowed to choose the regiment they'd like to join. A pal of Joe's talked about cycling battalions. Imagine, thought Walter, bicycling into battle, perhaps abroad, flying the flag with his comrades at his side. The brothers duly joined the 1/25th London Cycling Battalion, the most famous of them all.

Emma told them she was proud of her soldier boys and the girls looked forward to seeing them in khaki. The sons of many of her neighbours had already left home, their pink faces glowing with enthusiasm, inspired by the patriotic songs which filled the music halls – Marie Lloyd sang: *'I didn't like you much before you joined the army, John, but I do like you, cockie, now you've got yer khaki on.'*

While Walter was at home, waiting for his orders on when to report for duty, another young man was also waiting. Gavrilo Princip was shackled to the walls of a prison cell before being tried for assassinating Archduke Franz Ferdinand of Austria in Sarajevo on 28th June 1914, Bosnia's national day.

Bosnia had gone from one tottering empire to another when it was annexed in 1908 by the Austro-Hungarians from Turkey, a move which made the Serbs feel threatened. Gavrilo, born in Bosnia-Herzogovina, was a member of a South Slav nationalist organisation. He and his fellow conspirators had planned the assassination as the forerunner to freeing their country in favour of union with Serbia. Instead it set off a chain reaction among the jittery members of the Central Powers of Austro-Hungary and Germany on one side, and the Triple alliance of Russia, France and Britain on the other. The result was a war that was to last more than four years and see millions of soldiers and civilians dead.

Gavrilo was a small, sickly youth suffering from tuberculosis, but he was a good shot. He was among the crowds lining the route taken by the Archduke and his wife Sophie on a formal visit to the capital, stationed third in line to two other assassins from the melodramatically-named Black Hand Serbian nationalist group. The first failed to throw his bomb and the second missed. This caused a delay and slight change in the programme but when the Archduke's car hesitated at a corner, Gavrilo was still there. With two shots he killed both the Archduke and Sophie, his wife. As he took aim Sophie may have spotted him – she instantly flung herself across her husband in an attempt to save his life. The cyanide pill swallowed by

Gavrilo was out of date and only made him sick.

News of the assassination was in the British press next day but did not really hit the headlines. Probably a chum of the Kaiser's, thought Walter, turning to the page on county cricket.

The *Manchester Guardian* cosily reported that 'Archduke Frank Ferdinand had not played any great part in public life. He was by nature of a somewhat reserved disposition outside his own family, and was happiest when he could enjoy country solitude on his favourite estate of Konopischt. There he had a model farm, and he was quite an authority in all matters connected with agriculture.'

When the Austrians declared war on Serbia in retaliation, their ally Russia began to mobilise her troops, calling on the French to do the same. They needed little prompting.

In the meantime Germany declared war first on Russia, then on France, deciding to invade the latter first as an easier option than fighting the Russians. En route to

France, German troops poured into Belgium, using an invasion plan drawn up in 1905 when Edward VII was still trying to keep the peace between his cousins Wilhelm II and Czar Nicholas of Russia. But Edward had been dead for five years. Animosity, and armies, had built up enormously since then.

Although half the world was soon against her, Germany had huge resources: a professional army of 3.8 million men, ready to fight within a week of war breaking out, and a powerful navy whose U-boats were soon to take their toll of Allied shipping.

However, as they advanced on Paris, the Germans met more resistance than they had anticipated. The Belgians fought like tigers, the French were no pushover and then there were the British. The Kaiser had not expected the British to join the war and he, too, had thought it would have been won by Christmas, with a resounding victory for Germany.

A wet autumn followed the long hot summer. The fields the armies trudged through became quagmires. During the grim days of October and November, the French and British slogged it out with the Germans along the River Marne. Christmas was coming but there was no sign of an end to the hostilities.

Gavrilo Princip, under twenty when he committed his crime and therefore too young for the death penalty, was tried and sentenced to twenty years in prison at the grim fortress of Terezín, in what is now the Czech Republic. He was to survive until 1917 when he died, his tuberculosis complicated by injuries and the harsh conditions under which he was kept.

The Germans failed in their attempt to take Paris and the armies then turned north-east, coming face-to-face in Ypres in western Belgium. Young men on different sides were dug into trenches so close they could hear one another speak – or sing. In peacetime they would have met for a sing-song or game of cards and this, indeed, is what many of them did, crossing the narrow bar of no-man's land to exchange cigarettes or gifts of food sent from home, and joining in Christmas carols during a spontaneous truce. Many of them would soon be lying dead where they fell, so near to one another.

They gave their lives for causes which in a few hours turned them from natural-born friends into cold-blooded killers. This first Battle of Ypres cost Britain 58,155 men, the cream of her professional army. French losses reached 50,000 and 130,000 were lost by the Germans. Added to their casualties on the Russian front, where fighting had also been fierce, the cost to Germany in both manpower and morale was daunting.

Britain was still relying almost entirely on volunteers, who were wholeheartedly supported by most of the population. Any able-bodied man who hadn't joined up was in danger of being presented with a white feather, as a sign of cowardice, by a militant suffragette or a grieving parent who had lost a son.

There was hardship on the home front – fuel and food ran short. Cargoes of staple goods coming from the colonies and America were being sunk by U-boats and the distribution of local produce was disrupted. Emma preserved plums and summer fruits in sealed Kilner jars. She stored them at the back of the larder among Walter's favourite pickled onions and pots of dried beans. She and the girls peeled sour little apples from a friend's garden and cut them into rings which they threaded onto thin canes and hung them up to dry in the airing cupboard.

As the nights drew in, the popular tenor John McCormick sang Mr Ivor Novello's new song, *Keep the Home Fires Burning*. Ruby played it on the piano but she was not as musical as Mabel. 'She thumps the keys too hard,' complained Percy. Ruby took no notice. 'There's a silver lining,' she sang, 'Through the dark clouds shining. Turn the dark clouds inside out 'til the boys come home.'

Emma worried about Percy. He was very thin and that cough of his, much worse than Walter's, never seemed to get better. She had persuaded him not to volunteer for the army but he was still working much too hard now so many of his colleagues had left. She hoped, if conscription came, he would not have to go to war. Thank goodness Jack was safely in Australia, Horace was still only 15 and Joe and Walter were still in England. Jim, though, was in constant danger and the news from France got worse and worse. She jumped at any unexpected knock on the door in case it was one of the official forms every mother dreaded:

> *Sir,*
>
> *It is my painful duty to inform you that a report has been received from the War Office notifying the death of..*
> *No..........Rank.........Name.............. Regiment.......which occurred on the....................*
>
> *The report is to the effect that he was Killed in Action.*
>
> *By His Majesty's command I am to forward the enclosed messages of sympathy from Their gracious Majesties the King and Queen. I am at the same time to express the regret of the Army Council at the soldier's death in his Country's service.*
>
> *I am to add that any information that may be received as to the soldier's burial will in due course be communicated to you. A separate*

leaflet dealing more fully with the subject is enclosed.

I am......... Your obedient servant (signed) Officer in Charge of Records.

Emma must have rejoiced when Walter went to Devon, transferred to the Seventh Devons towards the end of 1914. There were rumours – there were always rumours – that the Germans had plans to attack the South Coast of England, but our Navy would protect it. Besides, as the last time England was invaded was in 1066, Emma was not unduly worried about her thirteenth child and Walter, cycling through the dark Devon lanes on his army-issue bike, wasn't worried either. In fact, he could hardly believe his luck.

4

A Near Miss

In spite of Emma's confidence, the government of Herbert Henry Asquith was seriously worried about an attack from the sea. Walter's cycling battalion patrolled the coast of southern England to look out for a German landing or fires started by enemy aircraft. Walter watched, but nothing happened.

There are few details of how he spent the first few months of the war. 'Tregonning & myself really meant to keep account from the beginning,' he says, 'But we never done so.' His resolve, as well as his grammar, was to improve and now, in the first of his two war diaries, he describes his experiences in Devon in 1915, taking up his pen during the last few hours of 1914.

This is the last night of the old year. I find myself unable to sleep so have lit the candle & taken out my diary to scribble down a few lines.

I wonder what dear old Jack is doing? Tomorrow he is to be married. I am sure he will be happy. Jeannie is such a nice girl I think. Good luck old boy & God bless you.

I have just looked out of the window at the night sky. The stars are shining, although a strong wind is howling down the chimney, a mournful noise. The ending of this disastrous year. I wonder what 1915 will bring?

Now I am feeling a little sleepy so will cuddle back to bed. Bed? Two blankets and an overcoat & a straw-filled sack.

Saturday, 2nd January 1915

Another year has gone, a year never in the ages of history to be forgotten. Is there not a little saying, 'The evil that men do lives after them,' etc. from Shakespeare?

Truly the evil that burst upon us in 1914 clouds all thoughts of 1915 being a happy one. With the dawn of this new year, the hand of death is snatching hundreds of our brave men's lives away whilst others lie in agony upon the battle field. As I looked out of my window this morning I could see the drizzling rain sweeping down the hillside, a poor outlook in itself.

But, natural optimist that he is, Walter soon cheers up:

Still, even rain brings a blessing for us Tommies. It prevents parades, hence our saying, 'Send it down David.'

Saturday afternoon: We have just been paid. The usual eight bob, they evidently don't give an annual rise of salary in the army.

On Sunday he goes to church with the battalion, the Totnes Band marching ahead of them, playing hymns: 'Onward Christian so-holjers, marching as to war…'

I do not like the sermon that the good rector preaches. He seems to think that we are dreadful sinners, the black sheep. Perhaps we are, but he seems to speak in a depressing way. Anyhow I did not feel, when I came out of church, much better spiritually. I wish Mr Hankinson had been in the pulpit. I always feel stronger and better after I have heard him, he seems to appeal to me in a far different way than this chap. This morning he asked us all to pray when we were going to bed tonight. Somehow I cannot imagine the whole battalion kneeling down by their bed sides. No doubt some will, but I do not feel earnest enough, myself.

For the next three days they are out at the crack of dawn doing tough physical exercises, running at the double up the hill to the parade ground.

As we ascend the hill, we leave the mist below us and the bright morning sun shines down on us. Two of our fellows have fainted, no doubt due to the cold & doubling-up on an empty stomach. It is not a rare occurrence.

I love these morning parades although my feet get awfully cold. It is a fine sight up on the hills – the sun shines on the frost, which glitters and sparkles like myriads of diamonds, and one can see the mist in the valley gradually lift as the sun plays upon it.

Then they get some news:

Tuesday, 5th January 1915

We have heard today that we are to go to the coast very shortly. Rumour has it that we are going to Torquay. Naturally we are all very excited. All sorts of wild tales are being spread about as to what we shall do etc. I hope that if they split up the company and send us on different stations that I shall be with Tregonning & the other boys belonging to our room.

Wednesday, 6th January 1915

This morning we had a jolly warm time of it on the parade ground. Somehow everything seemed to go wrong with drills & the Colour Sgt. seemed very much out of temper. During some of the orders I forgot to step up to the front rank when the about turn was given. Unfortunately for me the Colour Sgt. having no other way of giving vent to his feelings seized upon this incident as a means of doing so. As soon as the halt was given I was told to step out of the ranks, whereupon the Colour asked me if I had ever done any drill before. I said I think so. He came over to me saying 'Well cocker' (a word he always addressed us with), 'do you think you know what a blank file is?' I said that a blank file is a file that really is not a file, but the name given to the chap in the section that does two men's work. Whereupon he sent me back with a caution. Of course I said thank you Colour.

Thursday, 7th January 1915

This morning the rain is pouring down. Have come to Seymour Hall for lecture on musketry. I must say that St Major Tewins has a funny way of explaining himself. He starts something like this:

'Now then yer kin smoke melads but I won't 'ave any torkin! Now we 'ave ere a rifle and I am going through the parts of it. No torkin there, I got a nice job for anyone as I finds torkin – Now – we come to the bolt of a rifle and at the top of it we 'ave what we call the bolt head. Now on the bolt head we 'ave a little clip what is called the hextractor. Now why is it called the hextractor? Because it hextracs the cartridge. Remember heverfing is named after the fing it does. Thus we 'ave the trigger guard. Why is it called the trigger guard? Because it guards the trigger,' & so on. It was really amusing to hear him ramble on, anyhow it passed away the morning.

Friday, 8th January 1915

This morning have asked for two days leave. Have been to orderly room & received my pass from the colonel, & half fare ticket.

Tregonning has also got a pass for 3 days.

Have rushed back to billets & hurriedly packed my kit. It will be the first time I have seen mother since last October.

Tregonning & I just off to the station. If there were any taxis here I should certainly have one to convey Tre and myself to the station in pomp. I feel this to be a grand occasion. I shall be quite proud to go home in the uniform of His Majesty's soldiers.

There are no diary entries for Walter's home visit and when he returns to Totnes he has other preoccupations:

Monday, 11th January 1915

Arrived here 10.20 minus my kit bag & cardigan jacket. What a nuisance. I discovered my loss when I changed trains at Newton Abbott.

Went to parcels office & tipped the chap there to ring through to Plymouth about it. I might get it sooner or later. Hope so at any rate. Too tired to write anything else.

Tuesday, 12th January 1915

Have just discovered that we are to move to Paignton tomorrow. Tregonning is going to Torquay so I shall not be with him as I hoped.

But, not for the last time, plans are changed at the last minute.

After parade this morning our Captain told us that we shall not go to Paignton until next Monday. We are all much annoyed at this, and not a few of us indulged in a good flow of regimental language to relieve our feelings.

During these few days of enforced idleness, Walter's thoughts turn back to the home leave he had anticipated with such pleasure. Perhaps his short visit was a bit of an anticlimax; the older children were not around, the younger ones were preoccupied with their own lives and Emma was as busy as ever. Jim was home on sick leave but had no eyes for anyone but Dorrie and had been the focus of his mother's attention.

Walter writes the following entry with the restlessness of a young man away from home, aching with nostalgia but beginning to feel he no longer has a part to play in family life:

I do wish I had had a little longer leave when home. Although the little time I did have I must be thankful for. They all seem well although dear Mother could look stronger than she does. I went round to visit Mr

Hindley. He is just as ever, merry and bright. I wish I could go of an evening & have the old chats we used to have before this war.

Tuesday, 13th January 1915

It has been raining all day. The rain seems to sweep down in sheets & looks like a mist. It must be awful on Dartmoor on a day like this. The big gusts of wind tear along the valley in which Totnes lies, rattling the windows & banging the doors in its fury. We bought half a cwt. of coal this morning and have made ourselves comfy. Tre & Jack have drawn their beds round the fire this afternoon & now both are wrapt in sleep. There is little else to do. In fact considering that there are 30 fellows in this house it is very quiet, except for one room where they are passing the time singing various songs. I have got one or two letters to answer & am making the best I can of the coal box for a desk and the floor for a seat.

I awoke this morning shivering with cold. Found that Tre has collared the blankets & in his sleep has rolled over on the floor (lucky for him there are only a few inches between the palliasse and the floor) & has taken the blankets with him. Outside it is still raining, a steady downpour. The wind seems to have died down. The river is up very high this morning & already half the field at the bottom of the garden is flooded. By the look of the heavy sky I should think that the rain has come to stay. There is to be a kit inspection this morning. We are very busy trying to make our room tidy, arranging the few pictures that we have (chiefly cuttings from 'Punch') and decorating the grate with some coloured paper. Already our kit is laid out 'à la militaire' & we await the inspection by the Adjutant. 'Everything correct,' except one of my buttons undone (not a trouser-button though).

'Show a leg there! Show a leg!'

'Alri' Sergeant, what's the weather?'

For answer the door banged & the Sergeant strode down the passage, calling out parrot-like phrases in a high-pitched voice. Tre was already up & going through his morning ablutions when I jumped out of bed.

'Still raining? What's doing today Tre?'

'Scrubbing out billets, I think!'

'D....it, I believe it is my turn,' said I.

'Oh it's your turn right enough,' said Tre, 'The bucket & brush are outside the door.'

'Well, they can stay there until I have had breakfast.'

'Number 4 room to do the stairs,' shouted the Sergeant.

''Ere Sgt. I am not made of cast iron,' I retorted.

'Then you can do the orderly room as well,' he replied.

I mumbled something about eight shillings a week, then strode out into the rain to the place where we have breakfast. 11 o'clock found me scrubbing away vigorously under the watchful eye of the most beloved Sergeant.

Saturday, 16th January 1915

This morning we were told that we are going to the coast next Monday. As before, Tre is going to Torquay & I am going to Paignton under Sergeant Lercum. If there is any Sergeant I do not like it is him. I have asked Captain if I could shift stations but he will not do so. However I have got a chum. Murphy is also going to Paignton, so I don't mind quite as much. The rain has cleared up today and the sun is shining quite strong.

I have been to the football fields this afternoon to see our company play against E company. The game was very exciting. In the first half E company scored one goal and I must admit that they deserved it. The second half found our 'Huzzars' in better trim, the slippery earth giving them an advantage over the heavier team of E company. In the end we drew one all.

Sunday, 17th January 1915

We have all been very busy packing our kit bags this afternoon, cramming one thing on top of another, it is astonishing what one can crowd into these kit bags: blankets, boots, soap, shirts, trousers, hair-brushes and goodness knows what, that find their way into the various corners of the bag. We shall say goodbye to Totnes tomorrow for some little time.

Monday, 18th January 1915

9pm: At last I have a few minutes to spare. We arrived at Paignton about 1 o'clock this afternoon on our cycles.

A fully kitted-out army bike had a rifle slung between handlebars and saddle. A sturdy grey rubber tool bag was buckled to the cross-bar. Walter kept his for years.

In 1914, the army deployed 14,000 cyclists around the country, a number which grew to 20,000 by the end of the war. However bicycles were eventually abandoned as a means of military transport because they became hopelessly bogged down in the muddy fields of Flanders and were an encumbrance in the trenches.

After having a good dinner at the Temperance Hotel we went to the station for our kit bags & took them to our billets (some empty rooms above a wine shop). We then took our empty palliasses to the railway goods yard & filled them with straw. As soon as I had taken my bed to my room, I was told to go on sentry duty, & had to stick around on the pier head from 2.30 until 6.30. Am dead tired.

Have got to turn out again at 2 o'clock in the morning for patrol duty so shall turn into bed now. From what I can see from the present state of affairs, we poor beggers will have to do six hours night duty & six hours day. Not much time to ourselves.

All this morning I have been asleep. I only had five hours sleep last night. I have a room at the top of the house which is shared by Murphy (my chum) & the Sergeant. By the way the Sergeant is very amiable towards Murphy & myself & today I have helped him with the patrol check. I shall try and keep the right side of him, it certainly will make things more pleasant.

The Sergeant's amiability is to be seriously put to the test a week or two later:

The window of our room which is at the back of the house looks right down on the roofs of the houses in the neighbouring streets. (Our house has four storeys & is very high.) There are two other rooms on this floor, one we use as a store for our coal & odds & ends, & in the other room the rest of the boys sleep. Four in number.

Wednesday, 20th January 1915

We are really very fortunate in securing the Temperance Hotel as our place for meals & I cannot speak too highly of the quality & quantity of the food provided for us today. This new departure in life seems a little strange to me yet, but no doubt I shall enjoy it. One has a feeling of responsibility (the sort of feeling that perhaps a city policeman has) & also a sense of freedom after the discipline we were subjected to at Totnes. Of course, we have no drills, all our time is taken up on patrol.

Paignton itself is a jolly place, very clean with a certain charm about the whole town. At present it is filled with R.A.M.C (Royal Army Medical Corps) men, 'the idols of all the girls', so that at present our little section raises but small interest in the Paigntonians, but we shall soon get to know a few people, eh! What!

Thursday, 21st January 1915

Murphy has proposed this morning (I don't mean to a girl) having a deck chair, a table & a few other little things in our room to brighten the show up a bit. Of course I readily agreed with him, so I am to go to his home with him to help bring along some of the furniture. (Murphy lives not far from our billets & is himself a Paigntonian.)

This afternoon we have been very busy. We made two journeys to & from Murphy's house & to the billets & now have made our room look quite cosy. We have some little coloured curtains at the window. A nice deck chair & a table & a nice little rug. All we want now are a few good pictures on the walls to make the room look complete.

Friday, 22nd January 1915

I have just a few minutes to scribble down a few lines in my diary before I go on patrol. If any one could only see what clothing I had on they would think I was equipped for the North Pole. I have: 1-vest 1-shirt 1-cardigan jacket (presumably the one he lost when he changed trains, or a replacement), *1-tunic 1-overcoat, a scarf & mittens & in my pocket a woollen sleeping helmet. I shall need all these though, for the nights are intensely cold & we have to stay on the end of the pier for four hours, exposed to all the winds & the sea tumbling and rolling all around. Last night I felt like an icicle, but I do not intend to feel like that tonight.*

Well, now I must be off to relieve the patrol which is out, so must say goodnight to pen & paper and the warmth of the fire which is blazing merrily in the hearth.

Saturday, 23rd January 1915

Again the time has come when I should make another entry in my book.

Last night on patrol I must say that I felt much more comfy although even with the clothing I had on, the keen winds sent quite a shiver down my back and Baker and I huddled up together on a seat at the pier head to keep one another warm.

From the pier at night one can see practically all the lights in Paignton & the shore lights of Torquay are also visible. It is very interesting to watch the various lights gradually dwindling away as the night creeps on, and to look out to sea at the lights of the ships as they pass over the waters. Sometimes one sees the lights of a destroyer coming into the bay, where she stops, & then one sees the flashing of her signalling lamps, sending a message to Berry Head, and then off again into the night she goes.

This morning the R.A.M.C had a Church Parade. They really march well & seem a fine set of fellows. There are not enough of our boys to parade so they walk to the church with the Sergeant.

I did not go to church myself, sat in our room with a book & my old pipe.

I wonder what they are doing at home? I can just imagine mother busily cooking etc. while Sue is cleaning up the bedrooms & strumming on the piano in turns. Jim & Dorrie would just be returning from church, & perhaps have gone into the dining room and are cuddling down into the depths of the arm chair. I wonder if they are thinking of me now?

Monday, 25th January 1915

This morning we have had very good news from the Lieutenant. The day patrol is to be knocked off & only night duties to be done. This will greatly relieve us, who are now overworked. Murphy & I have been to fetch a few pictures for our room today & I must say that our room looks very snug now that we have put the finishing touch to the walls.

The fire is burning very brightly, & Murphy is reading a novel & dozing in turns, sitting in the deck chair by the fireside.

Tuesday, 26th January 1915

The weather has been wretched today, cold & wet. The sort of weather that acts as a damper to one's spirits as well as clothes. It is such a day as this that one feels the benefit of a fairly comfortable room.

Night is now drawing on & the sun, which appeared for about half an hour, is fast setting behind a bank of thick black clouds, throwing a pale yellow light on the dripping roofs of the houses and the muddy streets below. Murphy has just lit the gas in our room & has drawn the blinds across the window, shutting out the dismal winter evening. In our room the fire is burning a fierce red & everything is as cosy as can be. I myself am very tired so shall turn in to bed, as I have to go on duty at 2 o'clock in the morning.

Wednesday, 27th January 1915

It is with rather a hesitating pen that I set down in my book the events of the early hours of this morning, for I came very, very near to putting an end to one poor chap's life, and thus marring my own.

It happened like this. I was called by the Sergeant at 1.30am to go on patrol. I arose very tired, & dressed, & then put on my equipment, taking five rounds of ammunition out of the pouches to load my rifle with. I then proceeded to load my rifle, closed up the bolt & released the trigger (after shutting the 'cut off', which prevents cartridges in the magazine entering into the breach) when, to my horror, the stillness of the night was broken by a loud explosion caused by one of my cartridges. For a second or two I did not know what to do & all I was conscious of was the resounding echo from the shot. I then realised what had happened & saw that the bullet had pierced the floor two inches from the Sergeant, who was sitting dazed upon the bed.

I shall never forget those few minutes. I smelt the smell of burnt powder & could see a little hole, drilled through the floor, towards the next house. The Sergeant was as frightened as I, indeed he had been two inches from death that night and God only knew where that bullet had finally stopped for I knew that *it would need three thicknesses of floor & ceiling to stop a bullet fired at such a close range.*

We lay quiet for a minute or two, but hearing no sound I concluded that the bullet had confined itself to our house. It was impossible to go to the downstairs rooms, as they were locked, to find the direction the bullet had taken.

Presumably Walter went on patrol as ordered, his rifle short of one bullet. If he went back to bed at all that night, I doubt whether he got much sleep.

Next morning the manager of the brewery which owned the premises came to examine the room below.

It appears that the bullet had pierced the ceiling, then gone into the wall, turned and embedded itself in the floor, where it had stopped. The manager was very good about the whole affair and asked that it should not be spoken of. As for the repairs to ceiling etc., he would have that done himself.

A very peculiar thing about this affair was that only one report was made by outside people of the sound of the shot. The policeman on duty did not hear anything at all, & even now does not know. The fault lay in the handling of the rifle when loading. Instead of pointing the muzzle upwards, towards the ceiling which would prevent a shot from entering the breach, I had pointed my rifle down to the floor & thus a shot had slipped into the breach unnoticed. I am very thankful that no one was injured & now I am waiting to hear what the Lieutenant will say when the report reaches him.

Walter makes no entry in his diary for the next two days.

5

Marking Time

After a couple of days of worry, the routine of army life takes Walter's mind off the shooting. He hears that he is to work at the Coastguard Station, taking telephone messages and helping where he can. When he arrives, conditions are not quite what he expects.

Saturday, 30th January 1915

I have been sent to the Coastguard Station & received my orders from Mr Welsh, the officer there, whom I found sweeping up a heap of rubbish in the office. I must say that the appearance of the interior of the Station was not what I had anticipated, for we were always told of the cleanliness of such places.

The floors were dirty; the brass-work dull, in fact the place could not be in a worse state. However, Mr Welsh says this is due to the 9th Hants, of whom a section was billeted there before our arrival, & who spent their time in playing cards etc. instead of clearing up, & even when they left did not attempt to clean away their rubbish. So I buckled to & helped him clean up the station & it was not very long before we had it quite spick and span. Mr Welsh is a typical Navy man & a jolly good chap.

The news Walter had been dreading arrives next day:

Sunday, 1st February 1915

This morning the Lieutenant called to see the Sergeant about the shooting affray, & of course I had to go before him. However he seemed very nice about it, & said that if possible he would hush up the whole affair, but he was afraid that he would have to report the matter at headquarters, in which case he would say a few words on my behalf. I was jolly pleased that he took it that way &

hope I shall not hear anything more about the affair. Truly I have had a lesson I am not likely to forget.

Much to Walter's relief, the incident is brushed under the carpet and Fortune continues to smile upon Emma's thirteenth child.

For the Allies, however, 1915 begins badly. There are huge losses at Gallipoli in Western Turkey, the sinking of the British transatlantic liner *Lusitania* by a German U-boat with the loss of 1,150 civilian passengers and crew, and the increasing horrors of trench warfare as France endures a long, wet winter. But for Walter, Tregonning, Murphy and the other young soldiers tucked away in South Devon, the greatest enemy is boredom: long hours of 'nothing much to do.' Between a lot of sitting around waiting for telephone calls and freezing cold watches on the pier, they're kept active by kit inspections, parades and hours of 'scrubbing out' before moving on to new towns. They read books, play cards, write letters, and make schoolboy fun of people in authority.

A letter arrives from Walter's sister Mabs. Like all his siblings, he is slightly in awe of the upwardly-mobile Mabel. 'I love to read her letters,' he says, 'Her descriptions of the charming scenery of Devon, which she has often visited, give an added interest to my surroundings.'

Teenagers can turn into bundles of energy once they are motivated and Walter is inspired. He continues:

Even at this time of the year the walks are beautiful & I love to roam over the Marldon Hills & look down at the view below. One can see all the broad blue stretch of the sea with the white fringes of waves breaking on the shore and, through the trees, the little town of Paignton, the roofs of the houses looking like mere red specks in the distance, whilst all around nature is just beginning to prepare to shake off her dark hood of winter. Here and there one can see a few ferns just beginning to send out their new shoots, truly a sign of the oncoming spring.

On 4th February, with the arrival of a parcel of goodies sent by Ruby, Walter suddenly finds himself 'very popular with everybody, at least they tell me I am a jolly decent chap & a very generous one (while the grub lasts)'.

This evening those of us who are not on duty have congregated around the fire in our room. There are five of us boys. Murphy & myself are the proud possessors of the two chairs while the other chaps have drawn the mattresses to the fire. We are about to begin a feed of the contents of my parcel together with those things the other fellers have brought with them, & I know that we shall do ample justice to them.

Wednesday, 3rd February 1915

To-day we are going to shift two beds to the Coastguard Station. The Sergeant already has his own bed here, as he does a six-hour telephone watch, & then can turn in for the rest of the night.

I think that most of us will make the Station our principal abode as it is directly on our beat & only a few yards from the pier. Tonight I shall have to do telephone watch, from 3am until 9am. There is really very little to do, we have very few calls of a night, but still one must keep awake, in case of anything happening, & although the time passes rather slowly, one has the benefit of a cosy room, with the fire burning brightly in the grate, & a book or two to read, compared to four hours spent in the cold streets & on the pier with the waves rolling underneath & the wind howling all around.

Thursday, 4th February 1915

To-day it is suggested that we put a little of our money together & buy some coffee etc. so that the man going on duty will have a hot drink before going out. This is readily taken up, & I have been given the money to buy the necessary articles. We have a kettle, which Murphy has brought down from home, & most of us have cups, so we only need the provisions. I have bought a bottle of Camp coffee & given an order for a pint of milk to be left daily for us at the Station.

The Sergeant still remains quite decent towards Murphy & myself, & up to the present has kept away from the public houses. It is very good that he does so, for at Totnes he used to be a regular customer at *one of those establishments & when an NCO is that way inclined it is not all honey for the privates.*

A gap in the diary follows. From now until May, only a few scribbled highlights give us a tantalizing glimpse into incidents Walter never fully describes.

Saturday, 6th February 1915
Girl at the cinema.

Saturday, 13th February 1915
Home for wedding.

Tuesday, 16th February 1915
Lost false teeth.

Wednesday, 17th February 1915
Return of same.

Friday, 5th March 1915
The poacher.

Monday, 8th March 1915
A call in the night.

Tuesday, 9th March 1915
What the dawn saw.

The wedding of 13th February was Ruby's. She's the sister who sends him food parcels. You'd think she'd deserve a better mention. Perhaps, with five sisters married already, it was not a particularly notable family event. Also, Joe Povey was a first cousin and although the Royal Family married close relatives with alarming regularity, the Barleys may have disapproved.

The end of Walter's visit coincides with the loss of his false teeth. False teeth? At the tender age of nineteen? Until I read his diary I had no idea! Did he leave them in a glass in the bathroom? Would Emma have recognized them as Walter's?

Teeth duly regained, he returns to Totnes and the mysterious goings-on at the beginning of March.

Life continues at a relaxed pace for the soldier boys. They enjoy the freedom of these days in Devon. Walter is charmed by violets and primroses tangled in the hedgerows. He learns how to recognise birdsong and leans out of the billet window where a blackbird sings in the twilight.

'Oh blackbird, what a boy you are,' he declaims, 'Blowing your bugle to that one sweet star... How you do blow it! And does she hear you, blackbird boy, so far? Or is it wasted breath?...' The other boys laugh, not unkindly. They are used to Walter's spontaneous snatches of poetry and verse by now.

News comes that they are to be on the move again, and Walter forgets about life on higher planes. The boys clean the mud from their boots and brighten up their brass buttons and buckles with a bit of spit and polish. But it's not enough. Standards have dropped and sterner discipline is about to be imposed.

Monday, 3rd May 1915

This morning we are to start for Seaton, & we have made due preparations for our long run. Our kits are all packed & ready for the transports & we are now awaiting an inspection from the Colonel.

At 10.30 the Major came and inspected us. He is very dissatisfied with our appearance, & has sent us all back for a clean-up, allowing us half an hour. All the fellows have their gear in their kit bags, so I don't know how they will manage to clean buttons etc.

Again we parade and this time the Colonel has come down. A lot of fellows who wanted shaving rushed to the barber, who did the best he could, although in a great hurry, & has left the mark of his razor on a good number of faces. However everything is all right now, & we shall soon start off.

Goodbye to Totnes once more, although for a short time.

Tuesday, 4th May 1915

We arrived at Seaton 10.30 last night, dusty, dirty & tired. My word we did have a day. We rode along quite well, until we reached a small place about ten miles from Honiton, where we were invited to the Lieutenant's house to dinner, or rather lunch. It was then about 3pm & the lunch consisted of bread and cheese and cyder which I must say was *not quite a substantial meal on which to end our journey.*

We left there about 4.15 after giving a few rousing cheers for our hosts. We all went along all right until we were within fifteen miles of Seaton. Then most of us boys began to feel tired, & to make matters worse, the night was creeping on, & only three or four chaps had any oil in their lamps. The consequence was that with the oncoming darkness the fellows on ahead became indistinct, making close riding almost impossible. Soon the night set in, & everything was dark. Then the fun began. We were descending a hill at a good rate. The fellows in front of me were shouting to us behind to ride carefully in case we ran into them. Someone would be riding along, when suddenly, a few feet in front, he would see another cyclist & he would apply his brakes to avoid collision when another chap behind, not knowing what he was doing, would ride smack into him, & one after the other would pile on top, shouting and quarrelling at their misfortunes. After three or four of these accidents we were halted by the Captain, & when the chaps got together once more we were told to ride about eight yards from one another. We then resumed our journey, at a snail's pace, until we were about two miles from Seaton. Here some of the chaps were nearly dead, & a few of them fell out of the ranks & crawled into the hedges, where they could be heard snoring like broken-winded horses.

When we finally reached Seaton there was only about a third of the company left. The others had either fallen out on the wayside, or were walking with their cycles, too tired to ride another inch.

The motor transport & a motorcyclist were sent to pick up these men, whilst we went to a restaurant to get supper, of which we were in great want. That night, we slept in the town hall.

It was a sight, there were lines of huddled men, dead asleep, some in their clothes, too tired even to divest themselves of their coats.

Tre & myself had managed to get our kits, & together had got our beds out, & turned in between the blankets. The following morning we were allocated to our stations – some of us were to stay at Seaton whilst others had *again to take to their cycles & go on to the outstations. Tre & my other two chums & myself are staying at Seaton. We have got a room to ourselves in an empty house & are to go to the café for food.*

There is a long gap in Walter's diary from now until August, with a few cryptic notes in May:

Wednesday, 5th May 1915
Mist on Beer Head.

Thursday, 6th May 1915
I am again lost.

Saturday, 8th May 1915
We meet 2 girls.

Yes? And then what! Who were the girls? Did Walter lead one of them into the verdant meadows and gather flowers for her? Did he scramble after her to lie in the grass on the cliff-top, watching the gulls wheeling overhead, Walter's scratchy khaki jacket against the soft skin of the girl's arm? Did their sweet, unformed thoughts float in invisible bubbles above their heads, only to drift away in the high blue sky? Oh, Walter, Walter, lead me to the altar... Oh, lovely girl with hair the colour of corn, we'd live in a cottage with a low thatched roof, a well in the garden and a pony in the field, and our children would unfurl around the door like pink roses while I tilled the red soil. But, but, but...

Walter has plenty of time for day-dreaming but there is no more mention of girls. Instead he lists 'drills', 'grub at café' and a picnic. He goes to the pictures, tries his hand at fishing, sporadically goes on duty to watch the coast and gets another parcel from Ruby.

In July he notes that he is stationed in Branscombe but he gives no more information, except that on the 29th he injures his ankle. Possibly while scrambling up the notoriously steep chalk cliffs above the village or leaping over a five-barred gate to escape an inquisitive herd of cows? His foot becomes infected.

Monday, 23rd August 1915

This morning the Colour Sergeant came in the transport for the kits of the men to be shifted back to Seaton. He noticed that I had a bad foot so I have got to go in with him. I am not sorry really. I am a little tired of Branscombe. I am to see the doctor tomorrow morning.

Coming into Seaton we nearly had an accident with another motor coming in the opposite direction. The road was very narrow, & at this spot it bends round, just like a half circle, consequently we could not see the other vehicle until it was nearly on us. Both motor drivers applied their brakes, & we managed to stop just inches away from each other. Quite a near squeak eh.

Tuesday, 24th August 1915

Have had my foot lanced to-day. The doctor & a nurse came. He then got out his implements of torture & I, poor unfortunate, had to sit down & watch him. However I stuck my old pipe in my mouth & took a good grip on both sides of my chair and awaited *events. The doctor now advanced, knife in hand, having got hot water etc. ready, & kneeling down just tickled my poor foot with the point of his knife, & then with a sudden jerk of his wrist, he cut the gathering in two. Still I clung desperately to the chair, as he applied some nearly boiling water to the wound, & I must say that did hurt. However, the job was soon finished & after bandaging my foot he promised to call & see me tomorrow.*

How could it be, Walter wondered, that waiting for five minutes for his foot to be lanced seemed to last for hours, while visits home passed in a flash and a walk with a girl on the cliff-top was over in the twinkling of an eye. Of course, he reasoned, other forces came into play, like the anticipation of pain. Later in the year, Einstein published his own much more sophisticated field equation of Walter's theory of relativity. It provoked new ways of viewing time and space and continues to make sense of new discoveries but, in 1915, Walter's concerns were more immediate:

Mrs Agland, who lives in the next house to our billets, has very kindly proposed to attend to my foot for me after to-day. The doctor has called & given instructions as to the bandages etc. To-night I am to go to the Wesley Hotel to do telephone duty.

Thursday, 26th August 1915

The telephone duty that I have to do at the Wesley Hotel is A One. I go over about 11 o'clock pm to the office. The office is very comfortably kitted up & has a fine couch, which is fitted up as a bed for me, i.e. one sheet spread over it & a nice soft pillow. For blankets I use my overcoat & small tunic. At 6.30am the chamber-maid wakes me, when she appears to clean out the room. Of course I do not undress properly, only divesting myself of boots, puttees and tunic. I am afraid that if I did someone might get a fright at 6.30 in the morning.

Friday, 27th August 1915

Nothing much to do to-day. Have been sitting at my window looking down at the people passing by & reading in turns.

This evening I went to Mrs Agland's to have my foot dressed, she is a very nice person, & has two nice little daughters. They remind me very much of Doris & Sylvia (daughters of Walter's sister Daisy and her husband Bert Handley, the former 'dirty urchin') *at 235 Pinner Rd. Mrs Agland was a very careful nurse & I never felt the slightest twinge whilst she bathed my foot. Before leaving she insisted on my having supper, & also wrapped up some cake for me to take away. It is really very kind of her & I think that one appreciates these kindnesses more when away from home & all that home means.*

In spite of being unable to hop on his bike and explore the countryside, Walter seems to get out and about and soon makes friends as he limps around the village. But time hangs heavily on his hands.

Saturday, 28th August 1915

To-day I have nothing to do.

I have taken a breather as far as the beach, with the aid of a stick lent to me by Mrs

Dimond, who keeps a shop opposite our billets & who is very kind towards all the boys. It is just these little kindnesses from outside people that help one to forget the bareness of our billets & the rough life of a Tommy for one cannot help feeling that the sacrifice of home comforts is appreciated by some even if others do think that one is 'but a common soldier', and thank goodness they are but few. Certainly in this sort of life one can fully know the truth of those few lines by Emma Wheeler Wilcox:

*So many gods,
So many breeds,
So many paths that wind and wind
While just the art of being kind
Is all this old world needs.*

This cheerful author's positive thinking helps to keep Walter's spirits up. 'Laugh and the world laughs with you, weep and you weep alone' is perhaps her most famous line. Walter was fascinated by her spiritual beliefs: 'As we think, act, and live here today, we build the structures of our homes in spirit realms after we leave earth, and we build karma for future lives, thousands of years to come, on this earth or other planets. Life will assume new dignity, and labour new interest for us, when we come to the knowledge that death is but a continuation of life and labour, in higher planes.'

Sunday, 29th August 1915

There has been the usual church parade this morning. Of course I did not go, & truly was not sorry for I do not like the services at the parish church, although the vicar sometimes preaches a good sermon. Coppleston came in this afternoon to see me. He is a good chap & very lively company, & has been three or four times & passed away an afternoon with me. I am able to dispense with the services of my stick, shall return it to Mrs Dimond tomorrow.

Saturday, 4th September 1915

The days of this week have been pretty much of a muchness. Each night I have been to Wesley Hotel on telephone duty.

Monday, 6th September 1915

The doctor came this morning & examined my foot which, he said, is going on fine, & that he need not come again, although I am still to keep it bandaged.

Saturday, 11th September 1915

I have been down for a bathe this afternoon, the first for nearly a month. My word the water was rough – some of the waves were nearly five feet high. I swam out a few yards however, but when I was swimming back I came in on top of a huge wave which broke on the beach & threw me like a pebble, bang on the stones, still I escaped unhurt but for the remaining time I contented myself with just lying down & letting the waves break over me.

Rough seas sometimes wash away the pebbles covering Seaton beach, revealing a long crescent of golden sand between the cliffs rising up on either side of the town. It is the start of the ancient Jurassic Park between Dorset and Devon. Walter came across plenty of ammonites, the giant flat, fossilised shells like rams' horns, some too heavy to lift, which tumbled down to the beach as wind and rough seas eroded the cliffs. He tried to imagine what the world was like millions of years ago, when the cliffs were below the sea. These shells were inhabited not by snails, but a type of carnivorous squid, stranded when the waters retreated.

Walter put his toe into a pool and felt the gentle pull of a sea anemone on his skin, like a tender kiss. He took a breath of the fresh sea air. With all its problems, 1915 was still a good time to be alive.

Sunday, 12th September 1915

Nothing much doing today, the usual church parade although I did not take part in that as I still am on the sick list.

Monday, 13th September 1915

I have finished the little painting for Mrs Agland, which I have been touching up.

Mrs Agland is delighted with it, & has taken me into the drawing room to see other paintings by friends & relatives. She has a good collection, & some of them hopelessly outclass mine. Mrs Agland's daughter, 'Myrtle', has asked me to draw something funny, if possible, in her autograph book. Of course one cannot say no to the fair sex & so I have brought the book with me.

Seaton had a thriving fishing harbour for hundreds of years, until the railways took its trade away and new residents arrived – incomers who enjoyed the sea air and the peace of the Devon countryside. By 1914 smart Victorian and Edwardian villas extended round the curve of the big bay and climbed up from the slopes to the cliffs on either side. One such villa provided a comfortable home for Mrs Agland and her two daughters. They would stroll down to the grassy lawns bordering the sea front and watch the horizon, hoping Kaiser Bill would not disturb their peaceful existence and that nice young soldier boys like Walter would not be summoned to France. While Myrtle read to her sister, Mrs Agland knitted and sighed. At least they could help them enjoy some home comforts before they were called to the battle-front.

Tuesday, 14th September 1915

To-day I am to start duty once again. I have had a good long spell from work; in fact I feel that a little physical exercise will do me good.

I am to do telephone work, if I may call it so, during the day, & have a clear night's rest.

The telephone hut is situated at the top of a high cliff about one and a half miles from Seaton, & a glorious view of the valley of the Ocke can be obtained from this spot.

But, once again, Walter has 'little to do but read or watch the golfers on the links, and that seems to me rather monotonous.'

My hours are from 8.30am until 1.30pm & again from 6.30pm until 8.00pm. Every other day I do an afternoon watch between 1.30 and 6.30pm.

Walter gives in to lethargy. He cannot even be bothered to write a diary entry for his twentieth birthday, 22nd September, and it's not until a week later and a change of location that he puts pen to paper once more.

Wednesday, 29th September 1915

Have arrived at Dunscombe Farm, Weston, a very solitary place. I think the nearest shop is about three miles away. We have good billets though, & good beds to sleep in which is a great consideration & there is always something to be done on a farm, so I think our time can be well employed.

The boys help where they can, when they are not patrolling the villages making sure no-one is indulging in activities banned under the Defence of the Realm Act. This was passed a few days after the outbreak of war and included buying binoculars, lighting bonfires, melting down gold or silver or writing letters abroad in invisible ink. They can't always spot villagers feeding their chickens on crusts of bread or small boys trespassing on the railway lines, but they do quickly reprimand anyone buying a round of watered-down beer in the pub unless, of course, they are included.

Walter soon makes friends with the farmer who is gloomy at the prospect of his workers being called up. They've been trying to persuade him to employ women as farm labourers, he says.

What was the world coming to? They'd be giving them the vote next!

There were six million men at war when the Women's Land Army was organised. Britain was struggling to keep going, but many traditional farmers were against women working on their farms. Representatives of The Board of Agriculture were sent to change their minds and by the end of 1917 there were more than 250,000 women working as farm labourers, with 20,000 in the Land Army.

Some forerunners of the women's Land Army are already helping out at Dunscombe. They are healthy and red-cheeked from the fresh air. When they meet, Walter greets them affably. Most of them do not talk to Tommies but a fat and friendly one shows him how to milk a cow. He soon gets the hang of it and gets up before dawn to help in the cowsheds. There's to be a dance locally and he wonders whether to invite her to come with him, but in the end decides she'd be too heavy to pedal home up the hills on the crossbar of his bicycle.

Not only are the young men missing from the countryside, horses have also gone to war, requisitioned from farms and stables, the large shire horses to draw artillery, the hacks and mules to take provisions to the front.

The hedges round Dunscombe grow higher with nobody to trim them, the thatch on the farmhouse roof takes on a moth-eaten appearance and the neat patchwork of fields begins to look unkempt.

Under the Defence of the Realm Act, nobody is allowed to talk in public about military matters. There are rumours, but nobody talks frankly. This is smuggling country, where secrecy and subterfuge are normal: 'Them that asks no questions, isn't told no lie. Watch the wall, my darling, when the gentlemen go by.'

For centuries past, donkey carts have hauled contraband French brandy up though the deep lanes to country houses hidden in the soft hills with no-one to see them but the owls and foxes.

The excise men are the enemy, more to be feared than the French in the past or the Germans now.

Monday, 11th October 1915

This evening one of the boys here brought a pair of boxing gloves to light, so I & four others went to a barn to commence a few friendly bouts. For light we had two candles & an acetylene cycle lamp & the effect was rather curious. The first two chaps commenced two eight-minute rounds, & it was funny to see them whirling and dodging about in the dim light, which threw all kinds of fantastic shadows over the walls. Of course I had to go through two bouts. In the first I came off well but in the second I had my match & at the end of the time I saw red, that is to say that the candle lights looked red instead of yellow. Still I shall have another go tomorrow.

Boxing was a good outlet for the boys' testosterone-charged energy. They had gone to war to fight, not to farm. And their next move, it was said, was to be a big one. The speculation took Walter's mind off another very low-key Christmas. No bells rang out, no light, no rejoicing. For many, a time of mourning. Walter did his best to decorate the billet with paper chains and stars cut out of newspapers.

'Very nice,' said Murphy, but his heart wasn't in it. He'd lost an uncle in Flanders.

6

Passage to India

The war in Europe was stretching Britain's resources in money, materials and manpower. The Empire had come to her aid and thousands of troops from Australia, Canada, India, New Zealand and South Africa had already given their lives for the honour of the mother country.

Between July and November 1915, while Walter was making his forays into the peaceful Devon countryside, the long, bitter Battle of the Somme accounted for 60,000 Allied lives and there was no sign of an end to the bloodshed. The thought that he might be sent to France and the trenches can't have been far from his mind.

He never dreamed that instability in the wider world would affect him. The Ottoman Empire under Turkey, crumbling but still powerful, the expansion of Russia into Central Asia, and the emergence of Germany as a colonial power, were an increasing threat to British interests as far away as India, the jewel in Britain's crown.

The Khyber and Bolan Passes, on the northwest frontier where Afghanistan borders what is now Pakistan, had been gateways for invasion since ancient times. Their control was vital and the Indian government, under Viceroy Lord Hardinge of Penshurst, called for a British territorial force to augment the scattered battalions of Gurka troops already trying to protect this remote, mountainous terrain.

Walter was sent to the wild foothills of the Hindu Kush as part of this force.

Early in 1916, he'd packed away his trusty bike and prepared to leave his homeland. Many of his good friends in the Devons, including Tregonning, were indeed sent to the fight in the Somme, but fortune smiled once more on Emma's thirteenth child. He and Joe, his older brother by 14 months, who by now was serving with him in the

1/25th Londons, left England on 3rd February 1916 for Bombay.

He sends a postcard to his mother before he leaves with the sort of request boys have always been sending home to their mothers:

1st 25th Londons
No. 1 Company
c/o GPO London

'My Dearest Mother,

'Above is our address. We leave camp tomorrow morning 3 o'clock for Plymouth to embark on the *Aquitania* for India. Will you please send on, as soon as possible, my two good flannel shirts and washing and socks as I have no change with me. And will you also send five or six shillings if you can spare it.

'Goodnight dear Mother and God bless you and all. Fondest love from Wally. Will write letter as soon as possible.'

Walter was wrong about the *Aquitania*. By the time he writes the promised letter, the ritzy cruise liner is on her way back from Gallipoli with the wounded occupying her staterooms, gazing up from their hospital beds at gilded cherubs adorning the ceilings. And Walter is among 2,500 troops crammed aboard His Majesty's Transport *Ceramic*, bound for Bombay via the Suez Canal. Originally designed as a one-class ship to carry 600 emigrants to Australia, she offers only the most basic accommodation. All Walter has to gaze at when he's trying to sleep is a row of metal rivets, inches from his nose. He spends as much time as he can on deck. At eighteen-and-a-half thousand tons and measuring 200 x 21 metres, the ship was one of the largest and fastest troop ships used in World War 1 and much more solid than her odd name suggests.

However uncomfortable the conditions, he has enjoyed being at sea, buffeting past the coast of Northern France, feeling the swell of the Atlantic as the ship altered her course to the south. He had felt a frisson of alarm when they left Devonport and found themselves out in the Channel, which a few months ago he had been observing from the safety of the shore. Out of habit, he scanned the horizon for enemy ships. As he confided to Joe, German U-boats were a constant threat and impossible to spot once they had submerged. The *Ceramic* would be a tempting target, out here in the open sea. Joe reassured him – the *Ceramic* could travel at 15 knots and he was sure she could outdistance a U-boat's torpedoes.

One of the best things about going to India, Walter reflected, was being reunited with Joe.

The grey February skies lift a little as they enter the Mediterranean and Walter finds a space on which to write a letter home.

The following is the first in a four-year correspondence between Walter and his mother Emma, neatly tucked away in the linen bag with his diaries and several more letters from after the war ended. They remained stowed away in the cardboard suitcase in various attics until Walter died and they found their way to me. Mostly written in ink on flimsy, lined paper, the letters are unedited unless the meaning is hard to understand or the writing illegible.

c/o GPO London *(On board 'HMT Ceramic')*
Feb 19th 1916

'My Dearest Mother,

'You will be pleased to hear that we have nearly completed our journey. Tonight we shall have passed through the Red Sea & entered the Indian Ocean. We have then 1,640 miles to travel to Bombay, which will take us about five days, & our long journey will be at an end. I am pleased to say that danger from the sea now being passed, I am able to write you a letter which will pass uncensored & therefore containing more detail.

'After leaving Plymouth we had been on the sea for nine days before touching port. I remember it was early Monday morning. Feb 14th. We awoke to find our ship anchored in Port Said (Egypt) & you can guess we were all very excited, not having been near land for so long. As soon as I was dressed I rushed on deck, with many other fellows, to view our new surroundings.

'On one side lay the town, with its many coloured houses and verandahs, its long avenues of trees & wide streets, along which a few natives were strolling in long, loose robes of bright colours, adding to the quaint prettiness of the town.

'On the other side lay the blue waters of the harbour, dotted over with boats filled with various fruits or highly coloured silks.

'The shouts of the natives in their boats, hawking their wares, mingled with the raucous cries of the gulls wheeling overhead.

'Further down the harbour many large ships were anchored & as day grew on the noise became more intense. The gulls continued to cry & the men to shout. Added to this were the shrill voices of many coolies loading up the ships, the whistle of the tugs, threading their way in & out of the merchant ships, & the clanking of cranes as they hauled huge bales of cargo on board. But even the noise & bustle was welcome to us, we had become so accustomed to the monotonous throbbing of the engines of our ship as she ploughed her way through the swishing waters. We were still in port when the red sun, dipping down below the blue edge of the ocean, gave way to the silvery light of the moon. The noisy hum of humanity had ceased. On the shore myriads of lights blinked through the gathering gloom whilst the lights on the mastheads of the ships threw fantastical lines of light upon the water. Now & again the silence was broken by the regular splash of an oar as a boat passed us going towards the shore.

'Bedtime being near, Joe & myself brought our hammocks on deck, slung them on some hooks by the side of the ship and were soon comfortably nestled beneath the blankets.

'We lay a few minutes wondering what you at home were doing, & recalling our past experiences when on the dear old coast of England. Then wishing each other goodnight we were soon fast asleep. I might mention that now the heat is so intense we find sleeping below deck very hot & close & naturally prefer the open deck where one gets the benefit of the cool night breezes. However on the following morning we left Port Said and steamed slowly through the harbour towards the Suez Canal. At the entrance to the canal stands a fine African building belonging to the Admiralty. Passing this we enter the canal, which is about 300 yards wide & 99 miles long, being cut through one long stretch of desert, both on the Egyptian & Arabian side.

'At first one passes a few marshes, where the sea creeps in at full tide, but this soon gives way to the vast, yellow stretches of desert. Owing to the size of our ship we were only able to proceed at a very limited speed. You will no doubt think that our voyage through the Suez was uninteresting, but on the contrary we saw many fine & impressive sights about which I will not write as there is a great likelihood of this letter being censored.

'On the second day we reached the end of the Canal & passed that very picturesque town 'Suez', with the huge barren hills & peaks as a background whilst the blue sea (the gulf of Suez) reflected the bright yellows and browns of its houses. There again were avenues of trees and many quaint dwellings. I think that 'Suez' is perhaps the prettiest town on the whole voyage. After leaving the Suez gulf we entered the Red Sea. By this time the heat was becoming unbearable & the awnings & extra ventilators were fixed, whilst night time became the scene of wild rushes to secure good places on the upper decks, where to swing hammocks.

'Last Sunday morning we entered the Indian Ocean after passing through the Red Sea, &

shall not see land again until we reach India. However we are now able to have concerts & sports etc. in the evening so the time passes very pleasantly.

'I have not received my letters from home yet, owing to the fact that no mail has been delivered, but we hope to receive them when we land, on Thursday.

'Since we have been in the Indian Ocean I have seen some very fine sunsets. The tones are exquisite & the effects so grand that I am afraid I could not convey to you any description that would help you to picture the grand sights of sunset when on the Indian O.

'Joe and myself unite in sending our best love to all, trusting you are all in best health,

'Your loving son, Walter

'PS We were inoculated twice last week & today I'm to be vaccinated.'

The *Ceramic*, having safely delivered Walter and Joe to Bombay, sails back to England. On her next voyage she outdistances a German torpedo boat firing at her in the English Channel.

7

Heat, dust and dysentery

Emma's determination to keep her offspring 'regular' with a weekly dose of castor oil had continued throughout their childhood. Bearing in mind that this was used to induce labour in pregnant women as well as a laxative, it is not surprising that the effects were dramatic. The end result for Walter was almost chronic constipation.

He had survived most of the long voyage from Devonport to Bombay with only an occasional dicky tummy, but on his arrival he succumbed to dysentery and was taken straight to hospital. Too ill to write, the letter he eventually sent to Emma does not survive; it is only through her reply that we learn he has been ill. We have no account of Walter's reaction to 'the city of dreams', a pity because, after three weeks at sea, stepping ashore in Bombay in the early 20th century must have been an unforgettable experience.

Others, of course, did write home. Not only troops and traders, indigo planters, civil servants and adventurers, but members of more unusual groups, unique to the time and place, such as the 'fishing fleet' – the young women who stood, pale and apprehensive on the quayside, before being swept up by friends or relatives to an unknown future as would-be brides of the many bachelors working in the colony. One of these remembers watching the 'amethyst islands suspended in the opalescent mists between the sea and the sky' drift slowly into view as her ship comes in. She is to find herself a nice husband and become a privileged but hard-working memsahib. Those who were not so lucky went home to England as 'returned empties'.

Did Walter stand on deck watching out for the islands on the morning of 24th February, 1916? Or was he groaning in his hammock, clutching his stomach? Harry Oke, another of the 1/25th Londons squeezed into the *Ceramic,* wrote that the 'opalescent mist' was so thick that the ship grounded in the shallow waters of the harbour and was stuck overnight. They docked at dawn to an eruption of colour and the clamour of hawkers and beggars.

Walter was not present at breakfast and the shirt-sleeve parade that morning but Harry was and he and his shipmates set off on a sightseeing route-march around the town, shocked by the sudden, raucous noise and the close proximity of unfamiliar smells, people and animals. Harry describes Bombay as being like the curate's egg, good in parts. 'The Public Buildings and European residences are fine,' he says, 'the streets wide and electric tramways all over the town – but Oriental, you can't get away from that.'

The fine buildings Harry was referring to would have been the bulky arch known as the Gateway to India and the Oval Maidan, the open space where there were, and still are, cricket grounds surrounded by colonial mansions. Did he and his companions feel nostalgia for home at the sight of the solid Victorian architecture of the Railway Station and the Rajabhai Clock Tower? Designed by Sir Gilbert Scott, like Big Ben in London, the tower was commissioned by millionaire businessman Premchand Roychand, who built it for his blind mother so she could tell when it was time for her meals. Its chimes included 'Rule Britannia' and 'Home Sweet Home', which I hope appealed to Mrs Roychand as much as to Harry and his friends.

As Prince of Wales, George V had visited Bombay in 1905 and laid the foundation stone for the impressive museum named after him. The Prince of Wales Museum is now the Chatrapati Shivaji Maharaj Vastu Sangrehalaya, but everyone knows where you mean. It was used as a hospital in World War 1. Perhaps Walter was taken there to be treated, a living patient rather than a relic of a bygone age, lying in one of the fine halls under its high, domed ceiling. We can only imagine.

Two days after arriving at Bombay the brigade is aboard a Grand Indian Peninsular Railway train en route for Bangalore. A journey which, says Harry Oke, 'absolutely baffled description. We spent three days and two nights on the train, having our grub at little wayside stations and very tightly packed, our eyes and mouths opening wider and wider with astonishment as the journey continued.

'I don't know how long we are here for,' he writes, 'or where they are going to send us. I will say that I've never been more comfortable since I joined the army.

'We've beds to sleep on, mattresses, pillows and everything we require.' He is intrigued by the appearance of the local people: 'The men shave the front half of their heads and let the back grow into a bun. Another thing that is an education in itself are the womenfolk. It would teach the average English girl the lesson of her life. The great outstanding feature is their carriage. They carry everything on their heads and the result this has on their figures and their walk is obvious. They are stately in the extreme.'

Emma has to wait three anxious months before she hears from Walter. Already concerned about Jim, back from the trenches where he was gassed, and her fragile eldest son Percy, she wonders whether her thirteenth child has completely recovered from his bout of dysentery. Is he taking care of himself?

The following, the earliest of Emma's surviving letters to Walter, is in reply to the missing one of his own. It is written in a firm, sloping hand with a vigour that belies her age of sixty-five.

27 Archibald Rd.
Tufnell Park
London N
April 21st, 1916

'My dearest Wallie,

'It seems so long since I wrote & so long since I had a letter from you. I had begun to get fidgety, but Joe has been so very good in giving me all the news possible, & I was quite relieved when I got your letter (Tuesday, I think).

'Today is Good Friday & I am staying in trying to get some of my numerous letters answered, but yours dear must have first attention. I am thankful to know you are well again, I expect you will have to be very careful for a long time in what you eat & drink, nice to know you can be taken care of and treated well. I expect, if it wasn't for the dreadful weak feeling you must have had you rather liked being in Hosptl. Eh dear! & the ride in the Motor, now don't be like that old Gent and bolt your food but very carefully masticate it well, saves a lot of stomach trouble.

'It was indeed a splendid experience for you both to have had such a fine journey of which you have both given me such a good description I could fancy I was with you & enjoyed all the news, & a laugh to think poor old Wal was done by a little Brownie, did Joe get off free? & then that wonderful train ride oh how delightful, how you must have enjoyed it, & I fancy you boys have seen such sights, well there is some recompense for all you do.

'Were you pleased to see his photo? & now dear do have a few done of yourself, as near the same as Joe's, so that I can have you my Boys in one long frame. I have all but you dear so don't delay.

'I expect you know Jamie is billeted at Richmond & is very comfortable. Rue, Joe & Dorrie have gone there today. I do hope Jim will get strong. He looks fine in his kilts.

'I hope they write & keep you informed of their doings. How did the cake arrive? But you must be careful of currants, I don't want you to have dysentery again it is so weakening.

'Percy went last night to Scotland & took such a splendid ring with him for his Betty. He is to stay till Monday, not long enough but a little rest. He looks so tired at times.

'The Tribunal have given him six months extension, with the right to appeal again. I thought they would have exempted him.

'Vidy is taking up another Housekeeper Place at Harrow, she goes some time next month but is coming to stay with me for the next fortnight, so must hope the weather keeps fine, then we shall be able to get out together. I can't get on very well without someone's arm to help me. I am glad today is fine & hope it will continue for Easter.

'Marjorie is staying here for the week, she asks me to give you her love. She is growing so tall, I am very so pleased to have her, she is such a dear child. Tomorrow, Saturday, I am to have Cousin Frank & his young Ladie & Sunday Ethel & family to stay over Monday. Susie & Winnie are wondering if their Canadians in Kilts will be up again. They were here last Sunday, or rather Saturday. Sunday morning Jim was able to get up in time to be here.

'Frank says they are all well, Louisa & Emmy are in the Arsenal as clerks, he thinks Bert (Hedges) has to join up the end of May & says he does not feel so sure of his place, as there is a report that all single fellows will be taken from the Arsenal & married ones will take their places, but I should hardly think they will interfere with men who are making munitions. How I do wish this war was ended.

'Have you any idea how long you may stop in India, or are there any reports that you may go elsewhere, but one thing I am thankful for is that you did not have to go to France.

'Am glad you hear from your old chum Tregonning & hope he has not had to go. It is so nice to keep a good friend, this year dear completes 50 years of unbroken friendship between Mrs Oxenham (Auntie Susie) & me. Half of that time she has been in N.Z. but her letters have always seemed part of herself & have been a blessing to me, so dear I know it is good to keep in touch with an old friend.

'Now there is another old friend asking after & wishing to be remembered to my Brave Boys. Old Lady Smith, she is living with a daughter at Southend on Sea & has just received old age pension, she writes me she is well & Happy.

'Now dear if there is anything you want me to do or send, be sure you say & again I thank you & Joe for your nice long letters, I expect you are like myself and have plenty of writing to do, so dear if you are writing to anyone at home ask them 'do give me the news', then you need only write me a little one. I do hope you have got proper underclothing, I am afraid the things you eventually got in the parcel were little use to you & I am wondering if the 10/- order was all right. I want you to send your regimental number please dear as I do not know it & I have to give it on a form to obtain Jamie's money or allowance.

'Good night dear & God bless & keep you both. With Fondest love & many kisses, ever your loving Mother, E Barley.'

This affectionate Easter letter crosses with the one from Walter below in which he informs her of everything a dutiful son should tell his mother.

He's making the best of life in Bangalore, but reading between the lines Emma will see he is out of sorts. He doesn't feel well, it is overpoweringly hot, he is hungry, he hasn't had a chance to make friends and the accommodation at Baird Barracks – long, low bungalows in which up to 50 men sleep – is a far cry from the billets he and Murphy had made so homely in Devon.

Harry Oke may have found it comfortable but there is no space to yourself except your bed. There are white ants and scorpions and the local Europeans ignore you.

On top of all this, he is, like any twenty-year-old far from home, missing his mum, bored and lonely.

1st 25th Londons
201 Platoon
Baird Barracks
Bangalore
India
April 5th, 1916

'Dearest Mother,

'Just a few lines before the mail leaves. I read in the March newspapers that snow still continues in England.

'I do hope that the cold does not affect you & that you are keeping well in spite of it. Out here we are doing everything to keep cool, for we are now experiencing the hot weather. The glass reads on an average about 100 degrees in the sun and about 96 in the shade at midday, which is quite low for India. But Bangalore is one of the coolest spots for miles around so we think ourselves quite lucky.

'We have now settled down to the regular routine of barrack life, & the extensive organisation of sports does quite a lot to fill up spare time in the evenings before dark.

'We rise at 6 o'clock in the mornings, & after having a bun & a cup of tea we parade for

Battalion drills at 6.25 & finish about 9.15. The remaining part of the morning we have lectures etc. inside our bungalows, the heat of the sun making work outside impossible.

'The afternoons we have to ourselves, to sleep, read or write, according to how we feel. We never feel energetic at that time of the day. At 5 o'clock we begin sports & can choose between hockey, football, swimming & running. These sports are compulsory & considered necessary in keeping one fit & free from the many illnesses which are quite easy to catch if one does not take precautions. We have quite a lot of intersection matches & much interest is thus added to the games. Yesterday all the troops in Bangalore paraded before the general in command & the sight was very impressive. With the native troops we numbered about 4,500 men. After the reading of the Proclamation of Lord Chelmsford the new Viceroy' (he had succeeded Lord Hardinge on 29th February), 'a salute from 31 guns was fired. Then followed the national anthem, played by the Hants band, & finally the march past the saluting base. When, at last, we returned to barracks, we were just like lumps of dripping, for we had been under a broiling sun for nearly two and a half hours.

'I must tell you that the 25ths have given a concert at the Bangalore Theatre. It was a great success. We really have some very good artists, a few were professional before the war, & everyone was quite satisfied with the performance, at least there were quite a few columns in the Bangalore papers in our favour.

'Joe played a solo, quite nicely, & also a few obbligatos to some of the songs. In consequence he has already had an engagement at a dance held here last week, but no doubt he will tell you about that himself. There is to be another concert tomorrow & by all accounts it is to be an even greater success than the first.

'Our company has permission to run a rambling club & we have already been on a few very interesting outings across country, & soon we hope to visit some of the temples nearby. So you see Mother dear we keep ourselves fairly occupied. Next week I hope to be sent to a rest camp in the hills, about two days journey from here. There are about fifteen fellows to be sent from our Battalion, although we are not sure whether we shall

all go as there are only vacancies for a certain number. However it was nice of our major to recommend me for a rest & of course a rest, in the army, is always to be welcomed.

'About Bangalore I can say little. There are a few wide streets with pretty bungalows & gardens on each side where the Europeans live. Then there is the "maidan" or parade ground outside our barracks. This parade ground is about one and a half miles long and quarter of a mile wide, & used on all big military occasions.

'On each side are the European shops & five or six churches, which complete the European quarter of Bangalore.

'The bazaar or native quarter lies behind our barracks & is composed of dirty little streets & smelly shops. It is here that we do most of our shopping in the way of shirts, sticks or other knickknacks. Bangalore City, with the native quarters, lies some two miles out & we are not allowed there so I cannot describe it to you.

'I heard the other day a quaint story of the origin of Bangalore. It went something like this.

'Many years ago, before Bangalore existed, an Indian Prince set out from his palace on a particular morning & had the misfortune to lose his way. All that day he roamed about & it was not until night fell that fortune favoured him in the shape of a light coming from a hut in the distance. He made his way towards it, & on approaching found a wrinkled old woman bending over a pot under which burnt a fire. He called to the old woman & asked that food should be given him. Whereupon the old woman gave him the beans which she had been cooking & he devoured them with great relish.

'After his meal, he was directed to the road which would take him back to the palace but before going the old woman told him that soon a large city would spring up round the land which he had roamed during that day. He replied that, if such were the case, it should be called 'The City of Beans', or 'Bangalore'. Years have proved the tale, & now a small well-tower has been erected where the hut was supposed to have been and from which a good view of Bangalore is obtained. Of course this may be purely legend, but as quite a lot of places have their own little stories attached to them, I thought perhaps you would like to hear this one.' (A British legend, surely? 'Beans' and 'Bang galore'? The association must belong to the English language.)

'Well Mother I have no other news (or stories) just now, except that Joe & myself are quite well.

'Give my love to all at home, & to dear old Ruby & Jo. With heaps & heaps of love & hundreds of kisses,

'Your loving son, Walter.

'PS. Please ask Jimmy to write to me. I will try & write to him & the girls next week.'

Walter tells us nothing about his companions: the soldiers with whom he shares his bungalow, the Indians or the expatriate British living nearby in the pretty town of Bangalore of which he can say so little.

Throughout India, the army was spread thinly and British soldiers did not mix with other Europeans. As Walter says, they were banned from local villages and the only Indians they saw were the low-caste servants who cleaned out the latrines and emptied pots. There was an assumption, on the part of most of Walter's and his mother's generations, that to be British, white, Anglo-Saxon and Protestant was a huge honour and responsibility. It was therefore second nature to be, however subconsciously, condescending to anyone not in this privileged position.

There was usually only a handful of British Officers in charge of hundreds of Indian troops (Walter notes that there are 4,200 native troops in Baird Barracks). The situation changed after the war. More Indian officers were introduced and some of the British found themselves in junior ranks.

He seldom strolls along the shady lanes of the European quarter where Home Counties accents drift across from open windows. He feels uncomfortable. Minus his bike and in his uniform, Walter is just another Tommy.

But it is not a bad life. He and Joe become enthusiastic cricketers. They play cards and read all they can. Joe continues to play his violin. He socialises with the other lads more than Walter who is still getting over the effects of his illness and who has, in any case, a more reflective nature. Sometimes he is like Rudyard Kipling's 'cat who walked by himself'.

When news filters through about what the Allied armies have been facing on other fronts, they realise how lucky they are.

In Mesopotamia, forty thousand starving British and Indian troops have surrendered to the Turks at Kut Al Amara in April, after a long siege on a bend of the river Tigris in what is described as the most ignominious defeat of British troops in World War One. On the Western Front the death toll is horrifying. Jim is affected by mustard gas in the trenches of Ypres. His rasping cough never leaves him. Other young men are traumatised, blinded and dying in ditches at the Battle of the Somme, while all around the churned-up fields, spring flowers wave in the wind. Hopes are raised by a new British invention, a machine-gun-proof vehicle code-named 'tank'. Unfortunately, it is not operational in time to prevent further enormous losses.

More demoralising news comes in June when Lord Kitchener is lost at sea.

To the boys at Baird Barracks, the only real enemy is boredom. One day is much like another and they are getting tired of the same old faces of their comrades in arms. They almost never see a woman.

The Brigade organises outings to some of the marvels of the old state of Mysore (now part of modern Karnakata) largely to keep them off the streets.

There is no evidence that, clean-living boys that they are, either Joe or Walter go off to the unofficial military bordellos. These existed everywhere and were tolerated as being better than 'going off into a field'. Deprivation led to the lustier young men fulfilling their needs where they could. There is one account of a soldier being hauled up for molesting a cow. The case was dismissed when the cow's lawyer admitted his client had been charged with being complicit in similar acts on previous occasions.

As he grows fitter, Walter's energies are increasingly absorbed by his growing interest in the legends and culture of India which fascinate him and overlap, as they still do, with life back in London.

One of the most attractive artefacts from the area, 'Tipu's Tyger', is now a highly popular exhibit at London's Victoria & Albert Museum.

In September 1916, the first Zeppelin is shot down over London. Tanks are finally used to good effect in the Somme. And Walter has his 21st birthday.

There is no kindly Mrs Agland to knit him a scarf, no pretty daughters to ask him to do sketches in their autograph books and no retired villagers to invite him round to tea. He is nearly five thousand miles from home. But he is feeling much better and finally beginning to enjoy himself.

lst 25 Londons
Baird Bks. Bangalore.
Friday

'My Dear Mother,

'I find that I shall be unable to write a letter to you this week, so am sending it with this note by Joe.

'Yesterday I went to Kolar Gold Fields. They are the richest in India, & I had a jolly good time.

'I shall write a great big letter next week all about the goldfields.'

(If Walter does send this letter, it is missing. The ancient mine was closed in 2001 when old-fashioned methods of extraction made it uneconomical, but it is due to be re-opened at the time of writing.)

'I must add that next Monday morning we start out for three days of manoeuvres returning on the Wednes. night but I will get your letter written before I go.

'Joe & I received such a jolly letter from dear old Alan & Lily. Alan tells us that he is making great 'assaults' on the greenfly in the garden, & that instead of using gas he is trying "soft soap".

'Now Joe is waiting to seal up his letter. I must say tat-ta.'

The following letter from Joe mentions the *Londoner*, the regimental house journal which is almost as eagerly awaited by the soldiers as letters from home.

Cpl. J Barley
H Corp No 1 Platoon
1/25 London Rgt.
Bangalore
India
3 Oct 16

'My Dearest Mother,

'Just a line to let you know I am still going strong and Walter too is also quite well.

'Now Ma I am really sending you off that parcel I promised you, I am sorry I have not sent it before but I know you will forgive the delay.

'This week the Batt. have edited their first edition of the Londoner, it is not bad for the first attempt and I guess they will improve on it as they go along. I am also sending you a copy as I thought you would like to see it.

'This week we are changing quarters with the Hants Regt. and are going to Barracks again leaving the tents and sand behind us at Hebbal.

'I am sending back two of Horace's letters which I expect you would like to have back again.

'I saw Walter's letter you sent him and am now looking forward to receiving one for me.

'How did you enjoy your holidays. I trust they have done you good and that you are feeling quite fit.

'Last week we went for a night route march; we went 20 miles over rough country falling here and there over stones and ruts.

'I had been busy all day and was playing at the Bowring Institute just until ten o'clock pm. so you can guess I was pretty tired when we started off at 11.30pm. Well I guess

I don't want to do another one under such circumstances.'

This elite, members-only club, with rolling lawns, luxurious guest accommodation and fifty meeting rooms, was founded in 1868. It is still going strong.

'Please mother excuse this short note but as it's moving day I haven't much time to myself.
'Love to all, your loving son Joe.'

The heat abates and early rain dampens down the dust. Army life carries on. Late in November, the 1/25th Londons hear that that they are to be transferred to the Northwest Frontier, travelling more than two thousand miles by train to Burhan, in the Punjab, North West of Delhi.

There is a buzz of excitement among the boys in Bangalore. The crows rattle into flight above the dusty maidan. Walter looks at the parade ground where he's spent so long standing to attention in the heat, longing to scratch his nose.

The idea of the North West Frontier revives his spirits. Action at last.

He dreamed of romance and danger, marching up the snowy foothills of the Himalayas, repelling incursions across the Afghan border and quelling uprisings. There were tales of mounted tribesmen, who knew the rugged countryside like the back of their hands, coming from nowhere, ferocious in their casually looped turbans and ragged sheepskins. They were after your rifle and would go to any lengths to steal it. You must never take your eyes off it. At night, you had to sleep with it chained to your waist, or make a rifle-shaped indentation for it in your bed.

For all his twenty-one years and two summers of toughening up as a soldier, Walter was taken aback when Joe told him, 'You wouldn't want to be wounded and left behind after battle. The tribesmen would peg you to the ground, stick a piece of wood in your mouth so you couldn't swallow, then the women...'

'If they captured me,' interrupted Walter, 'I'd give 'em what for!' He thought for a moment. 'At least, I hope I would.'

He set to work, vigorously cleaning out the bungalow and packing his small number of possessions, and sang to himself as he went back to his day-dreams. He paused to look across the maidan. The crows had gone.

8

From Bombay to Burhan

Walter blew the dust off Emma's letters and tucked them safely into his kit bag.

He wasn't sorry to be saying goodbye to Bangalore. Not the place; the people. He was still smarting from the way the European community had ignored the arrival of the 1/25th Londons ten months previously.

'However,' he writes to Emma, 'We had quite a good send-off. Many of the fair sex had gathered to bid their friends farewell. I could not help thinking how different it was from the scene on the night of 28th February when we trooped out on to the platform, tired and travel worn. How greatly cheered we would have been, if only we had met with some sort of greeting from the white population. But except for a few people hidden away in the dark recesses of a gharry or a motor car, there was not a soul to be seen. And so we went on through the dark, dusty road, tired & dispirited.

'It was many weeks before these social snails, who live a life of ease and comfort, realised that our Brigade was not to be snubbed by people who owe their positions and safety to "Tommies" like us, but after a time we won our way & when we were leaving I am sure that Bangalore was really sorry to see us go.'

Walter is being hard on the 'social snails'.

He wouldn't have known it but 'hidden away in the dark recesses of a gharry' could have been another newcomer to India, a young woman seeing off a friend, feeling an estrangement from her surroundings far more profound than Walter's as she caught her last glimpse of a familiar face.

Perhaps she had been a member of the Fishing Fleet who had met and agreed to marry a suitable army officer or civil servant, and was now caught in a net from which there was no escape.

Many of these young women had been thrown into ex-patriate life straight from the comforts of a suburban home in England. A life where dust got into your eyes and your clothes. You were bitten by insects and caught horrible diseases which could kill you in a day. If you left your party shoes on the floor overnight they could be eaten down to the soles by morning.

Fine, there was the theatre, and the Bowring Club of course, where you could play cards and gossip, but you had to observe the strict hierarchy of club life or put up with bitchiness and back-biting. Your husband, whom you had scarcely got to know before you were married, was often away. Some women did good works and organised things, but the heat made one so lethargic. There were servants to look after the house and ayahs to look after the children until, if they survived beyond infancy, you faced sending them home to be educated. Some of the unhappy wives drank too much gin with their tonic water and fell into a decline, or the arms of someone else's husband.

It was advisable to drink tonic water, in those days high in quinine, to ward off malaria. The quinine was so bitter that a good slug of gin was needed to disguise its strong flavour. The gin was also supposed to be good for the kidneys and a twist of lemon helped to prevent scurvy if you were short of vegetables. It was a very acceptable way of helping the medicine go down.

The boys shouldered their kitbags and made their way along the platform to another adventure. The great engine was already puffing experimentally. Like a giant pair of lungs, it belched out clouds of white steam in anticipation of their six-day journey north. Walter felt a thrill of excitement.

'There was only one military car on our train, the rest being 3rd class native carriages,' he writes. 'Unfortunately for our platoon we were not the lucky ones. We had to make do with the latter accommodation. The native carriage is not made for comfort, or a long journey, having wooden seats, two very small wooden racks, & very badly lighted o' nights.

'Joe & I & three other fellows occupied one of these compartments, & I must say that after rifles, equipment & kit bags had been stowed away, there was not much room for five hefty boys. On the first evening of the journey we decided that two fellows could sleep on the floor & another two on the seats, but where the fifth was to sleep remained a puzzle, until one fellow hit upon an idea. The idea was to lash up a rug by means of stout cords tied through the ventilation in the carriage doors, thus forming a hammock.

'This we did, & it fell to the lot of the lightest of us to sleep therein. At first, the idea of sleeping in mid air, with a prospect of a sudden fall, didn't appeal to him, & it was only after we assured him that he would only fall on the fellow below, that he consented to climb into the hammock.'

Enclosed in the small carriage taking them to an unknown future, Walter felt the otherness of India as he never had before. This vast continent with its mix of culture, language and religion, its beauty and its poverty. So many of its people little better than slaves. There were very poor people at home in England, but at least they were British and had the King and the Labour

Party to look after them. And God was on their side. Or was there a deeper force which linked all races, all religions? Walter had begun to wonder. Once again, he wished Mr Hankinson had been there to advise him.

'Move over, Small Barley,' grumbled the lad wedged in beside him, 'Yer elbows ain't 'alf sharp.'

With such a huge brother in the same platoon (Joe was a good six feet tall, compared with Walter's five foot nine, and only then if he stood really straight), Walter soon became known as 'Small Barley'. This would eventually be shortened to 'Web', from his initials, and finally to 'Wee', an unfortunate nickname which stuck until he left India.

As the train steamed north, Walter peered out at a magical landscape.

'The journey itself was grand,' he recalls, '& the scenery varied, just as if one was passing through different countries. Great blue hills looked down on valleys rich with crops of tall Indian corn & rice fields, broken here & there by broad lakes on the edge of which could be seen banana plantations & tall palm groves beneath which nestled mud villages & little white shrines. In the evening, when the clouds had drawn a veil over the last pale gold of the departing sun, & the moon had cast her spell over hill & dale, a myriad fireflies would light their little lamps & dance through the trees, changing the scene into an enchanted fairyland. Often I was reminded of the song which you, Mother dear, used to sing to us when we were youngsters, Mrs Herman's *The Better Land.*'

Walter began to feel sleepy. Joe was already snoring. He wondered what the folks at home were doing now Christmas wasn't far away. His thoughts began to keep time with the rhythm of the wheels rattling on the track as night fell.

'I awoke on the morning of Dec. 2nd just before the sun had risen. The train had come to a standstill, & I popped my head out of the carriage window to get a glimpse at the sunrise & the fresh surroundings. Down the length of the train many other heads were showing out of the windows, asking their neighbours how they had spent the night, & rousing their chums, to get up & look at the sunrise, which was really grand. Slowly the big red ball rose above the peaks of the hills, chasing away the shadows on their slopes & in the valleys, & at length revealing a landscape of ranges of hills & vast plains, dotted with lakes, which reflected the light of the morning sun.

'Then we turned our attention to making beds, first shaking our blankets out of the windows & folding them & arranging them on the carriage seats for cushions.

'During that day we travelled through great tracts of jungle, overgrown with stumpy palms & creepers which grew in wild confusion. We also saw a variety of beautifully coloured birds & large, gorgeous butterflies. In the afternoon of Dec. 3rd we reached Dhoud, a junction 650 miles north of Bangalore, where we stopped for dinner.

'Our meals on the train were taken wherever opportunity afforded a good stop, so usually we ate at 10 o'clock in the morning and again at 6pm when we had an issue of bully beef, cheese & bread & butter (a very appetising meal after so much stew). We were also able to buy extras from a canteen on the train.

'After leaving Dhoud we made a good headway, the country now being flat & wooded, very like English scenery, except for a few cotton plantations which we passed now & again.'

Buffalo carts appeared from nowhere and ambled away into clouds of dust. Tiny, naked children ran beside the track, waving and pleading, until the train relentlessly left them behind. There were aspects of India that broke Walter's heart.

Gradually the dark shadows of flat-topped hills emerge from the starlit skies. The outline of a great fortress stretches across the high horizon as far as the eye can see. Couplings pull and squeak with the strain as the train begins to climb, the great engine puffing with exertion. The air is becoming cooler as the sky darkens into violet blue. Next morning they reach Itarsi Junction, where the wheels are checked and they take on a second engine.

'On the evening of Dec. 4th we began to climb the range of mountains just outside the town. The ascent is made by a series of big curves & the track is cut deep into the mountainside in places 40 feet deep. For two or three hours one is hemmed in by walls of rock & deafened by the grinding of wheels & puffing of the two powerful engines taking us up the steep gradient at about six miles an hour.

'It was unfortunate that we should make this part of the journey by night for the scenery, when one at last is at the top of the mountains, is really grand. As it was, the light of the moon enabled us to see the mighty forest, covering the hills below us like a great ocean. Sometimes we rattled over a deep chasm, which cut its way through the forest like a scar, looking very forbidding in the darkness. We noticed a chilliness in the air. Coming from the warm south as we had, it felt just like a frosty morning after one had hopped out of a warm bed.

'On Dec. 5th we reached the homeland of the once famous Rajputs. The many old, disused forts & walled-in villages bore testimony to the affrays they carried out against their enemies. That morning we reached Givalior. Givalior of old was built high up on a flat-topped hill, the sides of which are almost perpendicular. In its time it must have been a veritable Gibraltar. Here we were infested by a crowd of little boys, who offered us small bronze coins, only current in Rajputana, for one anna each. Considering that the coin was worth a farthing it was not bad business on their part. However we bought some just as curios to keep.

'We passed both Agra & Delhi that night. It was most disappointing to know that you were within short radius of one of the Seven Wonders of the World & not be able to see it. Agra, you know, possesses the Taj Mahal which is considered the most beautiful buildings in the world. The Hants Battalion arrived at Agra in the day time, & had a route march to the Taj Majal.

'We stayed in Delhi station for an hour or so, but beyond seeing the illuminated signs of a cinema & a few street lamps, we saw nothing of the great city, & that night we turned in beneath our blankets feeling rather sore. The next day we were making towards Lahore. We noticed that the people were very different from those of the south. The men are finely built & wear the baggy white trousers of the Mohammedans. They are altogether much finer in physique, & wear long black beards, although some dye their beards red, after their Prophet, which makes them look quite fierce. The villages also are different. Big & square, flat topped affairs, & a great improvement on the primitive dwellings of the South.

'We stayed at Lahore quite a long time, although were only allowed to play football, or walk about by the railway, so we saw nothing really to speak of.

'That night it was awfully cold. I slept in a jersey, besides having two sheets & two blankets to cover me. We passed through Rawl Pindi about dawn next morning & finally arrived at Burhan at 7.30am.

'And a worse place I have never been in.'

9

Hard Times

It was stuffy in the tent. Oh, for a breath of fresh air!

Walter undid the flap and crawled outside. The cold stung his cheeks. Adjusting his eyes to the pale moonlight, he looked across the dusty plain, a monotonous landscape broken by deep ravines stretching as far as the eye could see. Not a tree or any other living thing in sight.

It was hardly surprising that old Frontier hands called this part of the world 'The Grim'.

For a moment, the dust stirred and revealed a band of dark hills on the far horizon. Beyond them, to the northwest, lay Afghanistan. Further to the east a line of cloud, still tinged pink from the fading sunset, hung high in the heavens.

Was it really only cloud, etched so sharply against the sky? He looked harder. Perhaps it was just his imagination, or could it be a range of snow-capped mountains? The foothills of the Himalayas, whose highest peaks no man had ever climbed? He could feel his heart beating faster. Life on the North West Frontier might be grim, but what a thrill it was to be within sight of the world's mightiest mountains.

Burhan might not be such a bad place, after all.

'Wally,' called Joe, 'Come back inside, you're letting all the cold in.'

The camp fell silent. The moon cast great chasms of shadow across the plain. For an instant an almost palpable eddy of tension spread across the wilderness of the night, and was gone.

'Of course', Walter writes to Emma, 'We've got used to the dust & cold, for that is one thing we have to do, & altogether we have a fair time.

'You will be pleased to know that we have left behind our old friends the snakes & scorpions, & also that old enemy, the white ant, although we sometimes find him running around in search for boots etc. but not in the great numbers that we used to be pestered with in Bangalore.

'As may be expected, we have no monkeys or parrots up in this part of India, but we have any amount of jackals, a few wolves & hyenas, besides numbers of big rusty old ravens, a few vultures & the usual swarm of hawks. All these are very fit-looking creatures, considering the skeleton-like country in which they exist. The goats that roam about this district are peculiar to their kind. They all have very long coats, mostly black & brown, from which the famous Kashmir shawls are made.

'The means employed for travel over this bare, dusty land is the camel & it is a common sight to see a string of twenty or thirty of these ungainly beasts swinging along. We have recently been instructed in "loading camels" & we often have six of them on which we pile great bundles of tents, sometimes weighing well over 400 lbs, under the supervision of the instructor.

'Well, Mother dear, I must close my letter now as time is nearly up.'

Across the Afghan border in Kabul, 260 miles from where Walter lay sleeping, Turkish and German troops had been in occupation since 1915.

The British government of India was becoming increasingly jittery now that so many of the highly-trained forces forming the backbone of the Indian army were fighting in the trenches in Europe.

Added to the constant tribal raids from over the border was the threat of invasion.

There had been no choice but to enlist local tribesmen to fight on the side of the government. Most of them were Pathans, who did not conform easily to conventional army discipline. They were brave and resourceful and most of the time unquestioningly loyal to their officers. If one of them came across the body of a relative among the enemy they had just vanquished they would face the loss with equanimity. But occasionally the call of family and tribe was too strong and a young recruit would disappear with his rifle and a scanty but alarming knowledge of how the British fought.

This was the situation facing the 1/25ths. Well-drilled, resilient and eager for battle though they were, they knew they would be facing a very different foe from the Germans.

Attack marauding tribesmen with a large force and they would retreat into the hills and lie in wait to ambush you, biding their time until the terrain forced you to split into small units so they could hunt you down. Leave your equipment unattended and they would sabotage it. Go off on your own without a rifle and you'd find a knife at your throat. They would commit unspeakable acts upon your person, as Joe had warned.

Ethnically they were partly Aryan, possibly with traces of Greek blood from Alexander's soldiers in their veins. They were, it was said, expelled centuries ago from Persia.

Some had gone south and integrated with local populations, absorbing their cultures and religions. Those who had stayed in the Hindu Kush along the Afghan border, which included Burhan and is now part of the turbulent outer reaches of Pakistan, had fiercely maintained their identity, fighting to survive by raising goats and camels, and by plunder when they couldn't trade.

The only way to outwit them was to play them at their own game. And they had one weakness: they could carry provisions for only four days. With more manpower and resources, you could cut them off and defeat them. You looked and listened as never before. Patience and timing were skills that had to become second nature if you were to survive.

'From breakfast until tea-time, one is out scrambling over the hills. There is no let-up in our training.' Learning the tactics of guerrilla warfare gave Walter a buzz of excitement and he enjoyed the companionship of life under canvas.

With the arrival of Christmas, so long awaited, eagerly anticipated parcels were delivered in bulky mail-bags. To those watching them, as they were being dumped unceremoniously in the yard, the system looked chaotic, but just by writing the recipient's name, that of his platoon and 'GPO India', friends and relatives at home could be sure of post reaching their loved ones. It employed a simple form of recognition so efficient that it was used for military post during World War Two and after.

A parcel from Emma arrived. The cake it contained was as heavy with fruit as a bomb with shrapnel.

'The cake arrived with a tin of cigs, & nice letters from Miss Barmby and & Mrs Agland. Miss Barmby has sent me such a nice book, *The King's Highway* by J. Oxenham.'

Early on Christmas morning, a few tired voices began singing *The First Noel*. Walter's tent took up the descant and soon the carol rang out from the entire camp. But the hills still slept. They had known ancient religions from long before the arrival of Christianity.

On this day, in this lonely, wild place, religious differences didn't seem to matter. Walter felt an affinity to the entire human race, whatever its beliefs, and a little closer to heaven. He took comfort from John Oxenham's words:

> *In Christ there is no East or West,*
> *In Him no South or North;*
> *But one great fellowship of love*
> *Throughout the whole wide earth.*

At home in London, the fellowship of love between nations seemed remote as the impact of German U-boats sinking merchant shipping in the Channel took its toll. Shops were running out of basic commodities. Panic-buying caused even more shortages.

As she queued for basics like flour and sugar, Emma noticed the pinched, pale faces of wives and mothers gazing distractedly into the shop window. They were grieving for their lost boys and were too hard up to give the surviving members of their families a decent meal. If she offered them the meagre change from her own purchases, they'd be too proud to accept it.

With her inherent thrift and careful planning, Emma was able to stretch her resources to produce generous quantities of food for her family. 'For Christmas Dinner we had the usual Turkey & Ham,' she tells Walter. 'Percy bought the Bird & very nice it was & we all had some wine at Dinner Time & drank to our loved ones far away. We sent you our kisses & loving wishes & wondered if next Xmas would see you Boys round the table.'

Throughout the holiday Emma entertained a succession of friends, neighbours and relatives, listing them in a great outpouring of enthusiasm. Walter read and re-read every word.

'I had Daisy & the little ones & Vidy for Xmas Day & the week, then I had Ethel & Family for the next week also Lil & Alan for two or three Days & Mabs for one night & Marjorie for this last week, so you can tell dear: they all kept me pretty busy. Xmas Day was Happy & Quiet, we played cards in the evening with Doris & Sylvia & needless to say our thoughts were with you both during the day.

'Boxing Day all the Browns came to tea & we played cards & did some charades & had quite a lively time. During the holidays I treated Day, Ethel & all their chicks with Marjorie & myself to the Marlborough.' (An extravagant Edwardian theatre in the Holloway Road, demolished in 1962.) 'Cinderella was the Pantomime & very nice it was, quite simple & very prettily staged.

'Then Lillie treated Day & me to the Coliseum & Mabs is taking me somewhere, so you see dear boys it has taken up all my time, gadding about, & looking after the meals. Susie had five days off, so it made a nice holiday for her. Percy was kept very busy till after Xmas, but I was so glad to be able to have him at home for Xmas Day. Rue & Joe spent their Xmas at Boscastle Road but we had their company one evening when Lil & Alan were with us. Dorrie & Winnie have not seen much of them.

'Winnie is engaged now to her Canadian soldier Boy who has not gone to France, but remains somewhere on the coast as Telegraphist & Signaller. He seems quite a nice Boy. 22 I think. Also our Susie keeps up correspondence with Jack Edwards as Sweethearts. They will be married as soon as he can get leave. That is if, she says, she can save the money but he is in the trenches again & I don't think he will get leave easily. He wrote to me last week. I will put his letter in this.

'I am hoping to hear in your next letters that you got the second £1 safely, also that you both got the 10/- note as 5/- each Xmas present from me. I have just written to Doris & asked her to come up so that we can have a chat & read letters, then she will tell me when she is sending a parcel.

'I do hope that terrible dust won't hurt you, & take great care of yourselves dears for my sake. I was glad to hear you were to have a rest for Xmas, & hope the feed was good.

'PS: We, that is Lillian, Alan, Daisy, Vidy, Rue, Joe (Povey) & Sue, saw the Old Year out on Joe's doorstep. We had a merry walk home & met Percy & Smith on our own doorstep so we all came in & had Ginger Wine & cake & whisky to wish all a Happy New Year. Lots of people were outside. At one house just round the corner they were all in the garden singing, but there were no pipers.'

By the beginning of 1917 Londoners were faced with still more food shortages. Another menace, previously regarded as only a distant threat, now loomed overhead: Zeppelins.

The huge, cigar-shaped airships had increased their range since the previous summer and could now reach the centre of the city. Gliding overhead with an almost imperceptible purring of engines, they dropped their bombs without warning as people slept below.

'We're sitting ducks,' Emma told Sue, who was busy buttoning her boots by the fire, ready to go to work at the Arsenal. 'Hmn?' she mumbled. Her youngest daughter had her mind on whether Jack was going to ask her to marry him. She had moved out of Archibald Road to live with her aunt, Emma's sister 'Millie', who lived near the Arsenal in Woolwich. Enjoying her sense of independence, she wasn't too worried by the Zeppelins. If she'd known one was coming over, she'd have rushed out to join other excited Londoners gazing at the strange apparition.

The giant dirigibles turned out to be poor war machines; they only hit 10% of their targets. Filled with inflammable hydrogen, they were vulnerable to the incendiary bullets, quickly devised by the British to fire at them. Seeing them explode into a great ball of flame provided a spectacular, macabre thrill. Zeppelins were withdrawn later that year, to be replaced by something even more frightening, the great 'Gotha' bombers: each with a wingspan of 74 feet, they terrorised Londoners for the rest of the war like giant, death-dealing dragonflies.

Emma is determined to put on a brave face when Christmas is over, her guests have gone and worries beset her. 'I do hope this year may prove happy in the knowledge that you are coming home again,' she writes. 'I do miss you all so much, & now Percy is away it is worse than ever.'

Percy had joined the Honourable Artillery Company and was stationed at the Tower of London while he was training. In the early part of the war German spies had been executed there, a practice which so outraged public opinion that it was soon stopped.

'He says they are packing them off after seven weeks, but he seems rather to like it, & I think it will do him good. All the physical drills etc. If only he is lucky after. He says that they are well fed, clothed & housed, only the pillow was too hard and the first night he could not sleep. The next night he laid some of his kit under the bolster & it was O.K. He has slept away from home just a week, but manages to come in during the evening.

'They are dismissed from 5.00pm till 9.30pm. They are allowed 30/- per week until the civil liabilities settle what they will do, so that is good enough for me not to worry about Rent or Rates.'

Walter's next letter is slightly dog-eared, perhaps as a result of an arduous journey or because it was hastily folded in among other correspondence. As usual, because of censorship, there is no hint of where it was posted other than '1st 25th Londons, No. 1 Platoon, c/o G.P.O. India.'

'I was pleased to hear that Jim is well again & I pray God that he will be spared for you & all of us. I heard from 'Tre' last week (I am sending his letter to Mabs). He has had many narrow squeaks since he has been in France but has come through it all, unscathed. I hope that Susie likes her work at the Arsenal, & I am very pleased to hear that she is able to be with Auntie Millie, although you must miss her about the house.

'Has Kitty received the sandalwood box yet? I sent it last Nov 22nd & am rather afraid that it might have been on the 'Arabic' when it was sunk by a German submarine.

'Does Winnie ever pop in to see you? If so give her my love & best wishes for the New Year. I was so pleased to hear that Daisy & the chicks were with you for Xmas, & I hope that all are well. Please give my best love to dear Vidy & Percy.

'And here's a great big kiss and ever so much love for you Mother dear, for the present which you have put by for me, & I hope it will not be long before I can dispense with pen & ink & give you a real live hug & kiss.

'We had the news yesterday of America's attitude toward Germany, & although it is rather late in the day for America to come to any sort of decision, yet better late than never, & after all she is adding another link to the chain which will eventually bind Germany down & hasten the Peace for which the Allies are fighting.

'Yesterday a Mr Virgo, who is secretary of the English YMCA, came to Burhan. He gave a very encouraging speech, in the course of which he said that he brought a message to us from the King Emperor, and that he could safely say that all first line territorials in India would be home within four months of the end of the war and that is very cheering, is it not!'

This news, delivered directly by a messenger from the King himself, was an immense boost to the morale of the boys of the 1/25th. Convinced they'd soon be returning home, they returned with renewed energy to the routine of army manoeuvres, marching and camping out for the rest of the winter and early spring of 1917.

America would enter the war in April 1917, a few months after Germany had reneged on its undertaking not to attack passenger ships and sunk the Cunard liner *Lusitania*. The loss of 120 American passengers was enough to end Washington's previous indecision with the declaration by President Wilson that 'The World must be made safe for democracy.'

There is no more time to write letters, so Walter continues his story in a small, fat diary, *Collins' Indian Diary for 1917*, discovered years later among his correspondence in the linen bag. The ink is fading but Walter's hand flows confidently over faintly lined pages now as fragile as butterfly wings. These brief notes will remind him of his adventures once he's back in Burhan.

Saturday, 3rd February 1917

7.00am, load camels & mule transport.

9.15 leave camp 9.30 with camel transport with baggage guard.

Pass through Hassan Abdal Village market and mosque at top of hill. Arrive in plains surrounded by rugged hills and mtn. ranges. Here we are to camp.

Unload camels and help to erect the camp.

In afternoon we sleep although sometimes aroused to go on fatigue.

Sunday, 4th February 1917

Rest day. About 12 o'clock rumours that Kents and Sussex and Hants. Batts. are going up on to frontier on active service, great sensation. Further rumour denies that Kents are going but confirms the report of Hants and Sussex. Reports of rising in Baluchestan. Walked over to provision tent. Procured cakes & coffee.

Monday, 5th February 1917

We carry on. Early this morning we started on Brigade manoeuvres but returned to camp early in the afternoon where we heard more rumours of moving.

4.00pm: Great excitement prevails in our camp and that of the Hants next to us as an order is served to strike camp & proceed to take over those occupied by the Sussex & Kents. We struck camp & are awaiting orders.

8.00pm: Excitement abates. We are to sleep night in open.

Tuesday, 6th February 1917

Evidently mans are off. Sit about all morning in sun. Not any shelter & hot day. Feeling fed up.

2.30pm: Orders to start loading camels & mules.

Battalion parade at 6.30pm. Ready to march back to Burhan.

Burnt all fodder & straw before leaving.

Arrive at sunset, hunger unsatisfied and & tired out.

Wednesday, 7th February 1917

We learn that a rising of tribesmen raided a frontier station in Baluchestan last night. 19 men killed and rifles taken. Latest rumour states one officer & 17 men captured. Exploits by tribesmen amongst Indian villages. Expect if uprising continues we shall be off to the frontier.

10

Marching as to War

For the rest of that winter and the early spring of 1917 the Londons are involved in army manoeuvres, threading their way through the harsh terrain of the plain before making camp for the night.

There's a sense of adventure in Walter's letters to Emma. Even the gruelling routine of army life on the move is exciting when it involves loading camels:

'We get up at 7.30am. Parade for rifles at 7.35, get back to our tents, put up beds & make things tidy & get kit ready for transport, i.e. lay out a rug, with 2 blankets on top, with shirt, jersey, socks & ground sheet in centre & make up into a roll.

'At 8 o'clock we take the rolls (tied up) to camel transport. 8.05am breakfast, 8.30am parade and load up camels (16 bundles to each camel, making up the required load of 400 lbs. per camel).

'9 o'clock, clean rifles & make ready for parade. 9.15 fall in with full pack, consisting of overcoat, water bottle, haversack & entrenching tools, rifle & bayonet.

'And this is the work of two hours. However it is only the beginning of the day's work & at 9.30 the battalion is moving along beneath a cloud of dust. At the rear comes the mule & camel transport. From high ground you can see it curling along over the dusty soil, a mile & a half from end to end.'

The threat and thrill of fighting at the frontier still hang over them but Walter is more concerned with the day-to-day business of loading camels and mules.

The nearest they get to putting their manoeuvres into practice is a large-scale military exercise in early March:

'Last week we marched to "Jumna", a tiny village surrounded by great hills about six miles from Burhan.

'We rose at dawn & spent two crowded hours loading up camels and mules with all necessary bundles, a job taking not a little patience & nerve, especially where mules are concerned, for these four legged demons often take a distinct dislike to the loads imposed upon them.'

Walter loves animals. Since his days working in the dairy he has had an affinity with horses and has always been kind to smaller creatures. In India he has become accustomed to edging beetles and other bewildered insects out of his tent. Camels and mules are another matter but he has learned to regard them with weary tolerance.

'Suddenly when one is in the act of strapping on a load to Mr Mule, up will go his legs, down comes the load & off goes Mr Mule cutting all sorts of frisky capers in his delight at his freedom. However his freedom is only temporary & soon he is caught & held down by the ears & nostrils whilst the load is again placed into position & strapped firmly on.

'Fortunately the camel is not capable of such villainies, but still he is not always content to allow the 400 lbs. of load to be placed into position upon his saddle. Just as you are about to tie up the ropes holding the bundles in, up jumps Mr Camel in his awkward fashion, sending bundles sprawling in all directions & sometimes the unlucky loaders find themselves beneath the bundles meant for the camel. However we had everything in readiness by 7.30am & after snatching a hasty breakfast we got on our kits & paraded in the square. I was instructed to go with the camel transport, & so I went to where 150 camels were standing in rows, ready to move off.

'I soon found that I was to escort a string of six camels, & after seeing that the loads were all in proper order I sat down & waited for the signal to move. At 8 o'clock the Battalion marched out of camp, the long column looking quite picturesque in French grey shirts, khaki shorts & glittering brass buckles, until on reaching the trunk road, they disappeared in a thick cloud of dust.

'After the Battalion had gone, the mules filed out of camp & we had the order to move, & very soon a long line of camels with their great bulging loads was moving on down the path leading to the road. The camel transport moves very slowly, seldom faster than two miles an hour. Once out on the road the camels were arranged in files, one on each side of the road, so as to allow free passage to any other traffic, & it was our job to keep the camels close behind each other.

'Our route lay along the part of the trunk road leading to Hassan Abdal. The road here is straight for about five miles & is lined by an avenue of thin, leafless trees. On either side of the road are the plains, which stretch out to where ridges of rugged hills run parallel to the road. After travelling, or rather crawling along, for about two and a half hours, we reached the outskirts of Hassan Abdal. Here our column was delayed for some little time by crowds of yelling herdsmen driving their oxen to market, calling them with hoarse cries & beating them with short sticks, until they reached rows of rough stalls arranged beneath the trees at the roadside. Once they were tied up there was a deafening hubbub of crowds of excited natives selling & buying livestock. However, by this time we had turned round a bend in the road and had left the noise behind us.

'We had gone on for about half a mile when we reached the main village, its flat-roofed houses gleaming in the sunshine with dazzling clearness & the row of little shops sending forth all manner of odours, from burnt sugar & boiling fat to half-tanned ox hides which lay about the fronts of the shops beneath swarms of flies.'

At the time, Walter may not have realised how near he was to the site of the Hand of Guru Nanak, founder of the Sikh religion. But can it just be a coincidence that one of the best bed-time stories he used to tell my small brother and me was about a jealous holy man who tried to get the better of a visiting guru and his faithful minstrel?

Here is the legend: Once upon a time, Guru Nanak was resting after a long journey from a far-away land. He and his follower, B'hai Mardana, sang devotional songs of such beauty that very soon a crowd gathered, many of them disciples of Baba Wali Qandhair, the holy man who lived on the hill at Hassan Abdal. It was very hot and B'hai Mardana was thirsty after carrying his heavy stringed instrument such a long way. There was no fountain to be seen so the Guru suggested he should go to Wali Qandhair and ask him for water from his well. This B'hai Mardana did, explaining that he was thirsty, and respectfully asked for a drink of water.

But the holy man, annoyed at their attracting his followers, told him to go back and ask his own master for water. Down the hill went poor Mardana, back up and down again three times, getting thirstier and thirstier until he collapsed at the guru's feet. The guru realised a miracle was needed. 'Pick up a stone,' he told Mardana, and immediately a clear steam of cool water flowed from the dry earth beneath the stone. At the same time, the well on top of the hill dried up. The holy man was furious. He dislodged a boulder from the top of the hill and sent it rolling down towards the guru and B'hai Mardana but as it reached them, Guru Nanak reached out and stopped it with the palm of his hand. The impact was so great that it left the imprint on the rock. Wali Qandhair was so impressed by the miracle that he too became a devotee of the guru. The imprint of the hand remains in Hassan Abdal to this day.

Once clear of Hassan Abdal and its 'evil-smelling bazaars', the Battalion continues marching for a couple of hours before reaching a plain, surrounded by rugged hills and mountain ranges, where they find they are to camp alongside the Hants and two regiments of Gurkas.

Since the 1850s, when the Punjab was annexed by the British, several battalions of Gurkas had been based in Abbottabad, a hill station not far away. They remained there, patrolling the Northwest Frontier, until the partition of India and Pakistan in 1947. The town was named after Major James Abbott and achieved notoriety as the last hiding place of Osama bin Laden, leader of the terrorist organisation El Quaeda, who was killed there in 2011.

The hill station had a very fine panelled dining room with magnificent silver candlesticks. It would not have been out of place in an English stately home.

While the Gurkas' British officers are passing round the port, Walter and the newly arrived Londons are hard at work in the plain below, in a hurry to set up camp well before the sun goes down.

'We set to with pickaxes & spades to make a Perimeter Camp, always used by the Troops when fighting on the Frontier, whilst various parties were sent out to picket the surrounding hills. Even in practice, when one has just finished a march, making a Perimeter Fence is no light work.

'Each Battalion has a certain corner of the camp to make, & dig out the trenches etc.

'The four Battalions include the 2/8th Gurkas, 1/25th Londons, 1/9th Hants & Parano Gurkas. By the time the camp is finished it is a rectangular fortification crossed by two roads with gun emplacements at the corners.

'We had finished the trenches by 3pm & made the road in our camp & then we had to erect our "bivvies", the tents used when bivouacking. These are made by stringing together 2 groundsheets &, with the aid of 4 poles, forming a little tent, just large enough for three men to sleep under. We finished these & made preparations for sleeping by 4.30pm & then we sat down to dinner, which consisted of biscuits, bully beef, jam & tea. Joe & I were lucky that night as we had a tent to ourselves and we slept in our overcoats with four blankets over us, so we were nice & warm.

'Having just dropped off into a sound sleep (we were very tired) we heard a hurried order, calling softly to us to "Stand by." A party of Gurkas on the hills had made a sham attack on us, & already we could hear the pop, pop, pop of blank cartridges and the confused murmur of officers giving hurried instructions to the N.C.Os. Joe & I with all the other fellows scrambled out of bed, hastily put on our boots & equipment & rifles, which by the way we take to bed, & paraded by our tents. As soon as we were all up, we doubled into the trenches & lay waiting for a movement or sound from the enemy to give us the opportunity of lending him some lead.

'We lay in the trenches in total silence. Above us were the stars, twinkling down on us & on the dark blurred outline of the hills, on top of which lay our pickets, straining their eyes to watch the movements of the enemy. For many minutes nothing could be heard – all was completely quiet. Then all at once the popping of blank ammunition came from our pickets above us, & soon the hills were resounding with the noise of firing. Here & there a party of reserve men came charging up to the trenches, where they lay quiet. Still the firing went on from the hilltops & you could hear the echoes ringing up the valleys & the barking of the village dogs in the distance. And then all was quiet again. The "attack" had been driven off. Suddenly the bugle blared out "Cease fire" & again a more welcome note "Cease all operations", & we got up, stretched ourselves & returned to our tents, there to curl up beneath the warming blankets & to sleep & snore to our hearts' content.

'We were up again at 7 o'clock next morning, when the sun was rising, shining down on our little camp lying snugly beneath the great bare hills.

'Breakfast over, we commenced the day's work, which meant that we were to "attack" a certain village about four miles beyond. We attacked the village & imagined that we had burnt it & then fought our way back, firing at the enemy who existed only in one's imagination, & beating them, & so back to camp where we again made a royal feast of bully beef, biscuits, jam & tea.

'That evening Joe & I were with a party instructed to picket a certain small hillock, commanding the valley. We packed up our tents & made our rolls of blankets etc. Then we put on our equipment & overcoats, slung our rifles & shouldered the bundles, & thus burdened we set off to the hill.

'We arrived at the hill to find that at the summit was a Mohammedan cemetery. There was nothing else to do but to sleep amongst the graves. It was sunset when we put down our bundles & prepared our beds between the graves, which touched us on either side. However we had to sleep somewhere & that was the only place.

'On our picket we had to do sentry duty of 2 hours on & six hrs. off. Joe & I went on duty first & when we came off it was already dark & the gravestones looked quite weird in the light of the moon, but we were very sheltered & slept quite warm & unconcerned, although I haven't ever before slept in such a position. Indeed I have never dreamed that we should have to sleep in an Indian cemetery.

'Next morning we got back to camp, where everyone was bustling around getting things packed up for the return to Burhan. Finally when the camels & mules were loaded we began our march.

'Although I have described in former letters that our base camp at Burhan is not what one would call pleasant, yet one is only too glad to see the white tent tops on the grey earth after a few nights in the open. Since that event we have had another similar experience but as they are much of a muchness I will leave the relating of them until the day comes when we shall recount our adventures around the home fires with all the loved ones around us & the dear old homely roof above us & India as far away as we are now from you, Mother.

'Oh, how we all long & pray for that day, & perhaps it will not be long.

'Now Mother dear it is quite late & the jackals are already howling away, so that the hills re-echo their mournful cries. I must say ta ta for the present. Goodnight & God bless & keep you dear Mother.'

'Dear Mother' was getting worried. At least in Bangalore Walter and Joe were far away from any fighting. Now they were in the wilds of the North West Frontier with the prospect of hundreds of tribesmen bearing down from the mountains, charging across the plains on their camels, swords aloft, then sneaking up on their tents – anything might happen. 'Fancy having to take your rifles to bed with you, but I can tell you have to be very careful.'

In her next letter Emma mentions 'Dad' for the first time. She has never before referred to James in her letters to Walter, and Walter has never asked. Now he's shambling slowly into old age, Emma's tone is almost tender.

20th February 1917

'My dearest Wallie,

'I have had all the day to myself, so as soon as I had put things straight I sat down in my usual place in the kitchen & wrote to Joe. Dad went out about 10 & returned at 5. I have just given him his tea & Dinner together. He is quite well, but has had a bad cough.

'I was so glad to know the little gift I sent arrived in time to buy something for Xmas Day & that you & Joe spent the day happily with your chums & I pray you that next Xmas Day will see us all united at Home again, my word there will be some hugging & kissing going on then. I shall have to have a large bunch of Mistletoe, I never had any decorations this Xmas at all.

'I am so pleased you hear from your friend Tre, & that he is fortunate, please give him my best wishes, & tell him how glad I shall be to make him welcome if he comes to London. I think it is so good of those Devonshire Ladies to still think of & send to you. One lady told Mr Hankinson she always sends her Punch to you. Which one is that dear? But it is nice to know people have a good opinion of you.

'Yes dear Sue likes her work in the Arsenal, & does not seem to mind getting up at 5.30 & you soon hear her trotting about. She is earning good money & is setting herself up with clothes. Auntie Millie found it too much to do, with Sue as an addition & she rather wanted to keep the Bed free in case either of her Boys came home. Frank is still in the Arsenal & Fred is still at Salisbury. Bert is in one of the Shires, not far away, & Harry you know is in the Band of the Irish guards? They are all well.

'I gave Winnie your love, she comes down once or twice a week, & she sends her best wishes to you. She is busy always crocheting for her Bottom Drawer for I think she has made up her mind to go to Canada some day, so there is a pair of them, with Sue, who declared she is going, but I think it is far ahead anyway. I hope so, not that I don't like both their boys. They seem nice fellows but when I think of Jack, how cut off he seems from us all, I feel I don't want her to go & I am sure Jack's heart has ached many times to be with his Brothers & sisters. I feel even now he is trying to save enough money to come & see us all, of course if one has plenty of money, it makes everything very much easier.

'I have seen the beautiful Box you sent Kitty. It is indeed a nice present & I hope she will always keep it. She was here a fortnight ago for the weekend, but does not come round much.

'Harold & Mabs think to get married next September.' (Harold Povey is Emma's nephew and Mabs is a young neighbour, many of whom are called Mabs or Min or Sid or Lily or Walter. My father Walter has grown up with them all and eagerly devours every detail of Emma's latest gossip, hoping he will be home by the time his sister Sue gets married.)

'Min & Sid also I think are to be married this year but it is all off with Lillie Green & Walter. I expect Kitty has told you all that news eh! She told me she sent you a parcel but not what she sent. Hope dear you got tobacco, sweets etc. that I sent you in Joe's Parcel. & now I will close as I want to do some mending. With my fondest love & God bless you dear.

'Good night,

Ever your loving Mother,

E.B.'

Gallery

Sunset over St Pancras Hotel from the Pentonville Road 1884 by James O'Connor © London Museum.

Throughout the nineteenth century the Barley and Povey families were among the artisans and trades-people living and working in the Borough of St. Pancras. James and Emma started their married life in Somers Town, just to the north of St Pancras Station. Archibald Road, where Walter grew up, is about four miles away.

The Barley family, 1890 *(top)*. From left: Violet, James with Jack on his knee, Mabel, Lily, Gertie, Emma with Ruby on her knee, then Daisy. In front: Percy and Ethel. Still to come are Jim, Joe, Walter, Susie and Horace. Gracie had died in infancy four years earlier.

Young Walter *(detail, left)* partly obscured, as he often is in daily life, by his clever big sister Mabel.

The family in 1900 *(above)*. Walter and Percy back left, then Ruby and Jack. Susie aged three, stands on the left in front of Emma, followed by Mabel, Ethel, Violet, toddler Horace and James. Jim and Joe sit in front.

Cover of the London Opinion magazine *(top left)*, origin of the famous 'Britons, Lord Kitchener Wants You' recruitment poster by Alfred Leete.

Emma had already waved four of her sons off to War when this poster appeared in 1915 *(right)*. Now all she wanted was to have them safely home. © Imperial War Museum.

World War 1 issue bicycle *(above)*, toolkit strapped to the cross-bar, kitbag on the back, bedroll below the handlebars and an army rifle slung across the far side.

Instead of sailing to India on the luxury cruise ship Aquitania as he'd expected, Walter finds himself on the much more basic Ceramic *(top left)*. Once they reach the Indian Ocean they are 'able to have concerts & sports etc. in the evening so the time passes very pleasantly'.

A space for a bout of boxing has been cleared on the Ceramic's crowded deck *(top right)*.

One of the first sights to greet newly-arrived Tommies in Bombay *(above left)*, the Rajabai Clock Tower was designed, like Big Ben and the St Pancras Hotel, by Sir Gilbert Scott. Its chimes of 'Rule Britannia' peal across the nearby cricket ground.

Walter had his photo taken in army uniform in response to a request in a letter from Emma. The original has now disintegrated but this battered copy conveys something of his expression *(above right)*.

The boys of the 1/25th in Bangalore *(top)*. Walter stands rigidly to attention in his pith helmet, far right, third row from back. Brother Joe sits at ease below him, displaying his knees and puttees.

Joe with the violin James made for him *(right)*. His talent made him a popular army entertainer – at a concert at the Bangalore Theatre he 'played a solo, quite nicely, & also a few obbligatos to some of the songs'.

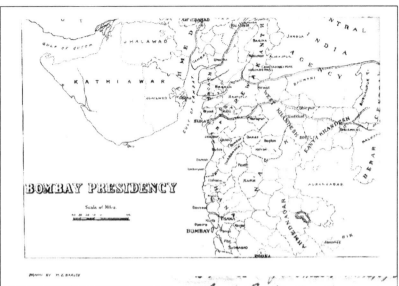

The only one of Walter's maps to survive *(above)*, drawn before his skills as a cartographer had fully developed.

He illustrates setting up camp with lively drawings in a later letter to Emma *(right)*. 'Each Battalion has a certain corner of the camp to make, & dig out the trenches etc…We had finished the trenches by 3 pm & made the road in our camp & then we had to erect our "bivvies", the tents used in bivouacking…& then we sat down to dinner which consisted of biscuits, bully beef, jam & tea.'

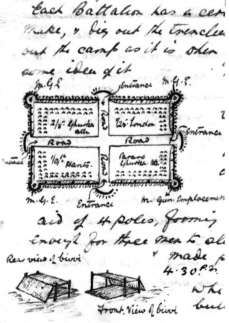

Sir Frederick Stanley Maude, KCB, CMG, DSO, born in Gibraltar, 1864 *(top left)*. Died of cholera in 1917 in Baghdad. 'His loss will be widely felt & regretted by all those who served under him out here.'

A palm-shaded courtyard at the Turkish Hospital in Baghdad *(top right)*. Walter is ill with dysentery again.

A lasting memory of Baghdad, *(above)* but the mosque is hard to identify. Walter's painting may have been done from memory when he returned to England. He has written on the back, 'Below are shops which, before the British Army took the City, were a covered-in bazaar. Note the broken arches. This was done by order of G.o.C. Maude to make a clear road through Baghdad for transport of army vehicles.'

Daisy's younger daughter Sylvia *(left)* poses in a nurse's uniform made by her sister Doris. The girls were keen supporters of the war effort.

James and Emma wait for their boys to come home *(top)*. James, tie awry, looks slightly the worse for wear while Emma sits resolutely on the far side of the fireplace.

Walter's easel *(above left)* served as the desk where he worked, painted and wrote letters throughout his life. It is still in the family.

Life is not all work and no play. On a climbing holiday in Austria, Walter is intrigued by a dance where you twirl your partner round to face you and plant a kiss on her cheek 'through the window'. As his sketch shows, when the boys are turned down by the local girls, they have to dance with one another *(above right)*.

The original painting of one of a series of advertisements Walter produced for Chilprufe children's underwear in 1921 *(above)*. 'Interview with Mr Hughes re appointment. Take Chilprufe layout. He seems satisfied…'

Jack and Jeanne got married in Auckland, New Zealand, on New Year's Day, 1915 *(right)*. Walter wrote in his journal, 'I am sure he will be happy. Jeannie is such a nice girl I think. Good luck old boy & God bless you.' Of the fourteen surviving Barley siblings, Violet was the only one never to marry.

Walter's Christmas card to Eileen, 1930.

11

In Alexander's Footsteps

'Last Sunday week,' Walter writes, 'I went with some of the old members of our Bangalore Rambling Club on a most interesting ramble. We travelled by train to Sarai Kala, & from there we walked to some old Greek cities which are at present being excavated.

'The cities of Taxila & Sarai Kala were the places where Alexander the Great & his army had their headquarters. The buildings are all "Grecian" & date back to 370 BC.'

This letter to Emma is undated but was probably written in late February 1917, one day 'when manoeuvres were off,' four years after large scale excavations began on the site under the auspices of the Government of British India.

Taxila, now part of Pakistan, covers a vast area where several ancient civilisations flourished and fell before being lost to the world for hundreds of years. At the confluence of three routes with Asia and the Middle East, it was in its time as fabled as Ninevah and Ba'albeck.

'As the excavation is not yet complete they have not been made known to the outside world. When it is finished, & papers & books are filled with the news of these newly found cities, it will give us great satisfaction to know that we were present whilst work was in progress.'

John Marshall continued with his excavations until 1935, revealing evidence of the subsequent Jain and Buddhist cultures which followed in Alexander's wake, as well as traces of earlier Persian and previous Hellenistic occupation. Even now, excavations are not complete. Recently-discovered Buddhist statues date from the Chandragupta Mauryan empire, when, after Alexander's conquest, Taxila had its heyday as a seat of learning and philosophy.

Knowledge was considered an end in itself, so important that its teachers charged no fees, there were no examinations and no degrees were awarded at its universities.

The site had been the scene of a cycle of hard-won empires that rose to power because of Taxila's enviable location and resources, each eventually conquered by other armies which developed as settlements with their own cultures, customs and beliefs.

Walter saw only the tip of the iceberg.

What had it been like, in Alexander's day, he wondered, as he gazed across a recently-cut trench to the wide expanse of strangely pitted land beyond it. Was that the tip of a pillar, just visible above a grassy hummock? One day, when the archaeologists had dug deeper, the world would know more.

What of Alexander's soldiers who, like him, had slept next to the earth in the wild hills of the Hindu Kush, living off the land or, if they were lucky, on the equivalent of jam, bully beef and biscuits? Constantly on edge in case of attack, they too were thrown together in that random brotherhood of a group that shares its moments of fear and elation.

The surge of adrenalin felt by Walter at the prospect of confronting the enemy and 'lending them some lead' would have been familiar to the Persians and the Greeks and to the Macedonians who thundered across the Northwest Frontier with Alexander the Great in the fourth century BC.

They met with fierce opposition, but Alexander paused for long enough during his campaigns to relax a little, perhaps playing an occasional game of chess. Or sending a letter to his mother, like Walter two thousand years later. For Alexander the emperor and Walter the soldier-boy, it was the only way of keeping in touch.

Alexander's style is confident, ebullient and indicative of his power. He writes, 'I am involved in the land of leonine and brave people, where every foot on the ground is like a well of steel confronting my soldiers. You have brought only one son into the world, but every one in this land can be called an Alexander.'

The blood of those who didn't die on the battlefield, who stayed behind when Alexander surged onwards in his quest to conquer the known world, still runs in the veins of their descendants, some of whom Walter encounters in the scattered villages of the Punjab as the Londons follow in their footsteps.

They had fought hard and long, Alexander's soldiers, sharing their young king's belief that the world ended on the east coast of the Indian continent.

Having conquered all in their path, they finally reached Taxila, and this is where Alexander met his match in 326 BC at the Battle of the River Hydaspes. The Hindu king Parvateshwar (Poros to the Greeks) ruled most of the area and staunchly defended the city. At the head of his vast army were soldiers mounted on 7,000 war elephants whose tusks were tipped with viper venom. They began to wreak havoc on the Macedonian army, but the elephants struggled in rising monsoon waters and in the end were no match for Alexander's infantry.

The two leaders conferred after the battle: Parvateshwara the vanquished king, tall and regal in his bearing, and Alexander the charismatic conqueror, short in stature, dressed like a common soldier, still with a limp from an injury at an earlier battle with Darius III, king of Persia. They instantly recognised one another's skills as soldiers and statesmen. When Alexander left, he appointed Parvateshwara his 'satrap', or viceroy. Taxila remained in Indo-Grecian hands before being destroyed by the Huns in the 5th century AD and abandoned.

Alexander prepared to continue his quest to the coast but his exhausted army had had enough. They had suffered enormous losses and their brilliant leader was showing signs of megalomania.

His mother, Olympias, convinced herself that the god of gods had sent a thunderbolt into her womb on her wedding night and that Zeus, not Philip, was his father. In spite of having been taught philosophy by Aristotle, who coined the phrase 'common sense', Alexander began to believe the myth himself.

After a final push, ending up in what was in Walter's time the city of Jullunder, Alexander gave up his dream and made his way to Mesopotamia and another fabled lost city, Babylon where, aged only 32, he died in mysterious circumstances in 323 BC.

Ethnic groups have shifted, religions changed and Taxila is once again a centre of culture. It became a World Heritage Site in 2007 and is now Pakistan's leading tourist attraction. Over the years, many of its treasures have been dispersed among the world's museums, many more having been lost or looted. Occasionally priceless objects are unearthed – such as the ring of Parvateshwara or Greek figurines cast in gold – and much still remains underground.

As future archaeologists re-examine those ancient ruins, will they also find a few vestiges of the brief visit a hundred years previously by Walter and the boys of the Bangalore Rambling Club? A coin, perhaps? A button or a pair of broken spectacles lost in the long grass? In search of history themselves, the Londons have become part of it.

Back at camp, there are rumours of a move. Nothing happens. The daily routine continues but the boys enjoy having some time off. Walter resumes his correspondence with Emma in a light, conversational style, very different from Alexander's tough rhetoric.

'We occupy ourselves by reading or bathing in a little pool just below our camp.

'Last Monday the Londons challenged the Hants Battalion in chess. Joe & I were amongst the London team. There were 40 tables & we all had a most interesting & enjoyable evening together. The Londons however carried the evening before them with a score of 35 games against 19 games for the Hants. Joe & I both won against our opponents. We are both getting on well with chess & represented A Company at Bangalore, where we had many good games.'

Activity intensifies when there's talk of an imminent move.

Sunday, 4th March 1917

About midday we heard strong rumours that the Hants, Kents & Sussex Bttlns. were going on service to the Frontier.

There was much cheering going on in the Hants lines, although the Londons felt a little down, being left in the cold.

About 4 o'clock in the afternoon we heard of a rising on the Frontier, one of our blockhouses had been rushed & a few raids into some villages had been effected by the hill men.

Monday, 5th March 1917

We rose early & already rumours were being circulated. We learnt that the Hants & Sussex were packing up ready to move away, although we had no news as to whether we should go as well.

That morning we hung about awaiting orders & at about 4pm we were ordered to strike camp. Great excitement prevailed & we cheered when every tent came toppling over, *for we really thought that we were to see some fighting at last.*

Brave words, but Walter was no battle-hungry warrior. He was patriotic enough to be prepared to die for his country, but was never put to the test.

Family and companionship meant more to him than promotion and power. Like Alexander, Walter was influenced by his strong-minded mother. Emma, though, was careful not to meddle in Walter's affairs. The domineering Olympias was divorced by Philip, who resented her interfering in politics. Also he didn't like her sleeping with snakes – she belonged to the cult of Dionysus, and this was one of the things they did, as well as drinking a lot of wine.

There had been no love lost between Alexander and his father Philip, a skilled soldier, fine statesman and successful politician, but a serial womaniser and aggressive drunkard. A smart remark by Alexander incurred such rage that he drew his sword with the intention of killing him. Had he not tripped over a carpet and fallen flat on his face, part of world history might have turned out differently.

Philip was murdered in 336 BC, probably at the instigation of Olympias and perhaps with the connivance of Alexander himself.

Emma would have had no truck with stories of such goings on so far back in history. James may have often had too much to drink and regularly beaten his boys but as far as we know he was not a womaniser – and rumours circulated by gossipy cousins that there was incest in the family are without foundation.

At times Emma may have felt like putting arsenic in his tea but as he grew old and surly in the company of his parrot, James was simply side-lined. She refers to him only twice in the entire correspondence between herself and Walter, and Walter never even mentions him.

'Your Dad is behaving himself,' she writes in her next letter, the nearest she gets to a suggestion that he might not always do so.

She is careful not to be over-protective of her thirteenth child, content to praise him and to tease him gently.

27 Archibald Road,
March 1917

'My dear Boy Wallie,

'Many thanks for your dear letters. I am going to take the one of your journey across India' (See Walter's letter in Chapter 8) 'to the School on Wednesday & read it to the Ladies while we are sewing. I know how much some of them will enjoy it. They very often ask after my Boys and you can certainly put a letter together.

'They have had little bits from time to time but this one is so good they must have it all. It is very good of you dear to give me so much time & news. The second letter is a dear little loving letter, which makes me know & feel that my Boys have not altered. They are just the same clean loving Boys that they have always been, & I thank God. No I did not remember that it was nearly a year ago that you arrived in India until you reminded me, but it all came back very real, it seems years since you have all gone, but as you say, dear, each week must bring you nearer home.

'Thanks for the nice Map. In my fancy I have taken that train ride myself. I am sending it for dear Jamie to look at, Jim wrote last week & was quite well. Dorrie is so good in sending things out to him, but sometimes she worries so till she is quite ill, poor kiddie she can't help it. It is a good thing Ernie has not had to join, or I think Mrs Hughes' (Dorrie's mother) 'would be crazy, & make Dorrie the same.

'The winter here has been very severe & it still continues to be very depressing, well we have the spring to look forward to, & as I keep pretty well I should not grumble, I have plenty of coals to keep a good fire & enough money to keep things going & a good home for my Boys to come back to, it is indeed a great blessing but for some it must be terrible. The poor Boys in France have suffered terribly.

'With the wet & cold & here in London it must be very hard for those with big families, for everything is double the price it used to be, & some things treble. Whatever should I have done at one time, if bread had been eleven pence for 4 pounds as it is now, & potatoes 2 pence a pound? I used to get 9 pounds for 6 pence. Are you just as fond of them as you used to be? & are they just as nice in India? But there dear, I won't begin asking questions. I see our dear Vera (Gertie's daughter, my father's niece, almost his contemporary) is asking enough, she is growing up to be a nice sensible girl.

'Percy does not think they will go anywhere safe, he quite expects to be in the thick of it all in a few weeks' time, he says they have hurried everything on so, they have been kept at it from early morning till almost bed time. Everything has been gone through. Bayonets, fighting & Gas tests, & Lectures by galore, after Tea, which they were bound to attend.

'I trust it may not be yet a while, that they have to go. I hope the news is mistaken, it would seem too dreadful. This is only his 9th week. If only he did not have go too. I am sure the outdoor life would be the making of him; he already looks so much better. He has had some nice photos taken. There will be one for you & Joe, I shall be able to send them next time I write.

'I am sure dear Vidy will be delighted with a photo & the Silk. I do hope it comes safe, it is so nice of you Boys to send it.

'I am saving all I can for you both, but you must tell me when you want some money.

'I do hope you will keep the brown skin. I should love to see you come home like Indians & with fierce moustaches. Now don't go & shave it off, it only makes it bristly & the girls like something soft.

'Don't forget to write to Mr Hankinson when you can. I don't mind if you skip me for once dearest.

'Now dear I must say goodbye for the present, with fondest love & kisses & God bless you.

'Your loving Mother, E.B.'

'PS: I am glad you remembered I used to sing "The Better Land", I used to like it very much. Now I never sing, only in Church.'

Walter does not keep the brown skin or the whiskers for long. As he tells Emma in a letter of 3rd June, they were not a success:

'I see you are quite interested in my little apology for a moustache, but so far from being a fierce Indian one it is such that even now I can muster only the proverbial 11-a-side, & very fair ones at that.

'Yes I still like a good share of "Murphys" although one cannot get those nice flowery ones here, so you see I shall like them more so, when I return, although @ 2d per lb, I should be rather inclined to put them in a glass case. Just think of the difference in prices out here to the present day prices in England. Here one can buy the best meat @ 3d per lb, and eggs are 3 annas per dozen. Best Butter from the Govt. Farms is 8d per lb & Tea is about 10d per lb. Whilst potatoes although of poor quality are 4 lbs an anna. & a chicken, ready cooked & served, costs about 1s2d, although in some parts of India they are as cheap as 8d. But then most chickens one buys in India are as tough as leather, whether they are natural deaths or not, that is always a mystery. One of the many mysteries of the East!'

The official daily food allowance for soldiers in 1917 was 1 lb 4 oz meat and 2 oz bacon,

1lb 4 oz bread, 2.5oz sugar, 2 oz oatmeal (for porridge), 2 oz cheese, 4 oz jam and 2 oz vegetables plus tea and salt. No wonder Walter is interested in the prices of food in local markets.

Late in March, a heat haze begins to shimmer in the dust over the camp. Exercises are curtailed, and there is little to do until, at last, they are given some news: a move is imminent! Walter may have heard it all before, but he notes optimistically in his diary:

Monday, 26th March 1917

Lieut. Saunders told us this morning that we should be going to Dalhousie very soon. The news was welcome to all, especially as the heat is getting strong.

12

On Top of the World

Lieutenant Saunders' promise comes true, much to Walter's relief, and they leave the barren plains of Burhan three weeks later. 'No longer do those deep ravines & great bare hills hold any terrors for us,' he writes, 'The days of mountain warfare training which took us through that land of greyness are past, at least until next winter.'

He tells Emma he'll send her a description of his journey through the beautiful hill country around Dalhousie, but the letter was either lost or never written. All we have is his diary.

Burhan, Monday, 16th April 1917

We have been hard at work all day, sweeping out the bungalow & putting everything in order. Our kits have been loaded on bullock carts, besides a number of E.P. tents – a very warm job.

The English Privates' tent had a support at each end and a pole across the top. It was made of multiple layers of white cloth, especially heavy when wet. It could accommodate 20 men or more. A number of them spread across a valley looked like a scene before a mediaeval battlefield. After they left, all that could be seen were brown rectangles in the flattened grass, worn to a square of earth where the soldiers had their last parade.

We had hardly finished our dinner when we were called to parade. We marched down to the station & on arrival there had to wait two hours for our train. We all had 2 bottles of soda water & a jam sandwich before starting.

The train puffs laboriously up steep tracks, lurching across iron bridges and rounding sharp bends. Walter can't resist leaning out of the window until smuts from the engine blow into his eyes and darkness falls. He settles down to sleep.

When they awake next morning the Punjab is behind them. They are now high in the countryside of Himachal Pradesh, about 50 miles from Dalhousie. There is little time to enjoy the pristine mountain air and admire the green valleys – ahead of them lies a gruelling, ten-day march.

Tuesday, 17th April 1917

We arrived in Pathankot after travelling all night. As soon as we got out of the train we had to unload 8 trucks of tents and stores and after that we marched to camp where we got a much-needed breakfast. I try to sleep but cannot as the flies are plaguing us. Went with Joe and others for a swim. From the river could see the Himalayas in the distance.

7.00pm load up transport. 2.15am start march to Dhar, 18 miles.

Wednesday, 18th April 1917

We reached Dhar at 7.00am. This march was really wonderful, the grand hills and deep gorges looking weird and fantastic in the darkness, although we were very glad to see the tents of Dhar peeping out of the wooded hill slopes. After a lovely wash in a stream we had breakfast and then we all went to sleep beneath the trees.

12 midnight we left Dhar and climbed up a steep winding road leading on to Dunera.

Thursday, 19th April 1917

About half way we halted & a few others & I lighted some candles and stuck them on some stones & by their light we ate a good lunch.

After this we continued the march through beautiful countryside. The black outlines of great ranges of mountains could be seen in the distance whilst below us, shrouded in a blackness unfathomable, opened a deep abyss. The sensation one experiences when marching along these mountain roads in the dead of night is quite uncanny.

Friday, 20th April 1917

6.00am we reached Dunera.

The rest camp and village are right down in a pretty valley between hills.

Whilst eating breakfast we had our photos taken by some enterprising wallah. Many camel caravans pass along the road which climbs the hill opposite us in a series of acute zig-zags. It is quite a sight to see them mounting higher and higher until they disappear from view,

Saturday, 21st-Sunday 22nd April 1917

Left Dunera 5.00pm yesterday, ascending the winding road in exquisite scenery. Great red hills rose up in picturesque buttresses with deep gorges cutting through them. Here and there immense pine forests broke the bareness of the scene, softening a scene of grandeur and splendour. As we marched on *we climbed steeply. On one side of our road soared steep rocky precipices whilst a deep chasm lay directly beneath us on the other side.*

Heavy black clouds gathered overhead as night fell, making everything so dark it was difficult to see our road. In some places we could not see at all, but all the time we could hear the water go splashing down some 600-800 feet below us. Flares were lighted soon after this although they did not assist much. Presently we entered a narrow cutting between two hills and stumbled into Nani Khand Rest Camp.

Walter is exhilarated by this life. Camping by streams, plunging into icy rivers at dawn and marching through magical scenery – he feels more alive, fit and fulfilled than ever before in his twenty-one years. Beyond every summit of every mountain another beckons. Remote villages perch dizzyingly on rock faces. Lush meadows are full of wild flowers and rhododendrons clamber up the slopes.

Around the hill station of Dalhousie itself improbable mock-Tudor cottages, imposing public buildings and solid English churches repose confidently in this cosy outpost of the British Empire. Dominating it all, mountains on a massive scale, fast-flowing rivers and dense forests of great deodar cedars, weeping conifers with feathery branches, like giant Christmas trees, reach up to the snows.

Not since he'd arrived in Burhan and looked across the plain to the distant snowy mountains had Walter felt such a sense of oneness with the world.

Rabindranath Tagore (1862-1941) the internationalist, anti-Colonial Bengali writer and philosopher and the first non-European to be awarded the Nobel Prize for Literature, completed his studies in Dalhousie after spending some time being educated in England. He was heralded as a man before his time, convinced that, eventually, 'each country in Asia will solve its own historical problems according to its strength, nature and needs, but the lamp they will each carry on their path to progress will converge to illuminate the common ray of knowledge.' The words to the Indian National Anthem are his:

The life that streams in joy through the dust of the earth in numberless blades of grass and breaks into tumultuous waves of leaves and flowers is the same life that is rocked in the ocean-cradle of birth and of death, in ebb and in flow. I feel my limbs are made glorious by the touch of this world of life.

>'Jana Gana Mana'.
>Rabindranath Tagore, 1861-1941

When Walter died a copy of Tagore's poems lay amongst a pile of his favourite books. The poet was a strong influence in his life as an adult as Fred Hankinson had been in his youth; in fact both Tagore and Hankinson shared many of the same ideals, their difference in race and religion proving no barrier to their common interests. They mixed in the same liberal circles and lectured to the same audiences. It is quite possible that they came across one another in London where, in 1913, Tagore met George Bernard Shaw.

St. George's Day, Monday, 23rd April 1917

Nani Khand is certainly the most picturesque place we have yet seen. The tents are pitched above a bridge spanning wild streams rushing down a jagged rock face. Straight out below us we can see the beautiful valley falling away in receding outlines until it is lost in the hills beyond. A little way down the mountain we can see the village, just a few scattered houses.

Tuesday, 24th April 1917

Arrived at Banikhet yesterday night at dusk in pouring rain. We had marched through clouds all the way. Had to change on arrival. No beds or bedding. Broke part of partition to make fire & stood around naked all night. The scenery and freshness of the air are beyond all praise & this morning the sun lighting up the cold blues and greys of the snowy mountains seemed to unfold to us a land unknown, so beautiful & tender after the plains.

Wednesday, 25th April 1917

We dried all our things & then went to top of a hill from where a most splendid view of Himalayas is seen. Met the head of the YMCA in his hut and sat on the verandah watching the effects of storm clouds gathering below & above the mountains.

Very grand and presently we were treated to terrific thunder & lightning which afterwards left everything covered with frozen snow.

Thursday, 26th April 1917

This morning every living thing in the outside world is sopping wet, the great drops glistening on the boughs of the trees like lovely jewels. The smell is delicious.

We were paid out today. The surroundings are so beautiful & magnificent & I feel so happy here. Joe and I slept in the corner of the hut.

To their surprise, within a few weeks of leaving Burhan the battalion is back, not on the dry plain they'd started from but, to their relief, in the Punjab, on the Eastern, fertile side of Himachal Pradesh. They arrive at Jullundar where they are to wait for more orders, with little idea of where they are to go next.

Jullundar was where the exhausted army of Alexander the Great turned back, shattering his dream of conquering the known world.

Walter, too, was glad to put his feet up after the vigorous march. Fascination with his new surroundings seems to have overcome any thoughts of homesickness as he writes to Emma:

'We spend the hot, languid hours of these early summer days in the large roomy bungalows at Jullundar. It is a small city, situated down on the vast plains stretching throughout the whole breadth & length of India. We are now about 230 miles S.E. of Burhan & 100 miles south of Lahore, & the nearest hill station is some 100 miles away, so that whether one looks north, south, east or west, there is nothing to be seen but the great rolling plain, relieved by avenues of trees & ripe barley fields & little Mohammedan villages, scenes presenting strong contrast to those at Burhan.

'It is a very hot station, dry in the months from May to September as are all the stations on the plains of the Punjab. The summer heat in this part of the country is usually 118 degrees (Fahrenheit) in the shade, indeed we are told that for a week or so during last summer the glass registered 125 degrees. All the white civilian population here, as well as at Lahore & Delhi & other stations, leave the cantonments in May & go up to the hills. Of course we have to stay here, & everything is done to obtain the maximum of ventilation in the Bungalows.

'Our bungalow is a long, two-storey building. The ground floor is divided into four large rooms, one for dining & recreation. A wide staircase in the centre of the building leads up to a fine wide verandah on the 1st floor, while on either side are wide glass doors leading onto two sleeping dormitories. In each dormitory are twelve large double doors, opening out onto the verandah, & over each bed there are large punkahs, which are worked during the hot summer nights by punkah wallahs or servant boys. The verandahs are 12 feet wide & are sheltered from the sun by large sliding lattices. In the summer months we are not allowed out of the bungalows from sunrise until sunset & wallahs or black servant boys do all the running about.

'Of course this sounds very nice & easy but one very soon gets fed up with sitting about in stifling heat. One must have exercise, & every kind of sport is encouraged during the early mornings & evenings, & even now hockey, tennis, football & cricket find many supporters, indeed one is really compelled to enter into one or more sports. Since I have been here I have taken up running & every evening I and another chap named Ferguson, nicknamed Pimple, go for a cross-country run for two or three miles. Last Thursday morning our platoon held a paper chase.

'We started out at 6.00am & had a very jolly run. The hares led us through all kinds of places, across corn fields, over cactus hedges, through half-awakened villages & over wide streams. When we at last finished in a field near our Bungalow we all agreed that we had had an exciting time.'

When Walter was growing up in London, Mr Hankinson had encouraged him to open his eyes to other religions and the philosophy and poetry of other nations. Since coming to India he'd thought about this a lot but at heart he still seems to hold what appear to us the endemically racist views of his generation. He would have been surprised to know how expressions like 'black servant boys' jar on today's reader, as does his attitude in the following paragraph:

'Just before we left Burhan we had a draft of 150 men from Blighty. They all come from the Hackney Rifles & what is more surprising they are nearly all Jews & have the characteristics of the chosen race & glory in such names as Rosenstein, Goldstein etc. etc. However like most Jews they are lucky, for they have all got 2 weeks' leave so that they can attend certain ceremonies held in a large Synagogue in Calcutta, a journey of 2,000 miles by rail.'

He has no cause to complain because he too, is lucky - good fortune seems to make a habit of smiling on him.

With no training at all, Walter could draw a straight line and an almost perfect circle freehand. If anyone in the family wanted a formal card or caption written or Emma needed a decorative border for a poem she'd copied the cry would be, 'Ask Wallie'. This was a time before computers and photocopiers so anyone who didn't want to go to the expense of getting something printed had to write and draw by hand, in pen and ink or pencil.

His talents can't have gone unnoticed in India and a short time after arriving in Jullunder Walter has some unexpected news.

Friday, 27th April 1917

This morning news comes that a chap named Reid and I are to leave here & go to Mesopotamia as litho draughtsmen.

He receives the news with mixed emotions. Baghdad had only just been captured from the Turks and he'll be in an even hotter country and in another desert. Worst of all, his big brother will be staying in India.

I do not know how I feel about it. I do not want to leave Joe. The job seems good and pay is better, however I have no choice.

Saturday, 28th April 1917

I went to the Station Staff officer today and arranged for passes etc. Walked around hillside in eve.

Sunday, 29th April 1917

Reid and I will leave early light tomorrow.

13

Turning Point

Walter admires his reflection in the carriage window as the dark, flat-topped hills flash by. High forehead, curly fair hair cut short at the back and sides. Neat ears. Not bad looking, he reckons, squashing his straight nose against the glass and smiling at his own vanity. His face hasn't really changed during his six months on the North West Frontier, except it's no longer a boy looking back at him through the flickering landscape. The deepening shadows beneath the cheekbones and the rugged set of the jaw belong to the face of a man.

He sighs. His reflection sighs back. It's been another long train journey, taking him away from Jullunder and Joe to a barracks a thousand miles away before he leaves India for ever.

'Barley!' someone calls from across the carriage. There's a pause before he realises they must mean him. He should have remembered there's no need for him to be called 'Wee' now he's the only Barley present.

The train rattles across the points as they draw into Poona, 120 miles south east of Bombay. Walter is stationed at the nearby army barracks at Kirkee 'for a spot of training' before sailing to Mesopotamia. He is a willing pupil and does well. 'I am now qualified as skilled,' he writes to Emma. 'Our work is very interesting, & is chiefly litho drawing & printing. Most of it is maps, although occasionally we have to do drawings of "dug outs" & earth works.'

The key event leading up to Walter's opportunity to develop his map-making skills and taking him from Northern India to Mesopotamia was the Seige of Kut Al-Amara, a small town on a marshy loop in the Tigris. The siege had lasted from December 1915 to April 1916 and has been described as 'the most abject capitulation in Britain's military history.'

At the outbreak of World War 1, Mesopotamia was still part of the Ottoman Empire that once stretched across the Middle East, the Arabian Peninsula, the North African Coast, most of the Adriatic coast and the islands of the eastern Mediterranean, even threatening the once-powerful city state of Venice. Its population included Slavs, Greeks, Turks, Arabs, Berbers, Kurds and Armenians. For the most part, its leaders let their subjects live as they chose, Muslims, Jews and Christians. However its territory had gradually been recaptured or lost as new nations emerged from within its boundaries. The empire had shrunk to what are now Turkey, the Middle East and much of the Arab coastline. The Ottomans abandoned their successful multicultural formula and instituted a policy of 'Turkification' that made Turkish the official language in schools, the army and government. This led to dissension, especially amongst the Arabs who made up about 60% of the empire's population.

Rebellion was encouraged by the British, whose charismatic liaison officer, named Thomas Edward Lawrence, would soon earn a place in history as Lawrence of Arabia.

The Turks made what seemed like an unlikely alliance with Germany, which like Turkey was seeking to prevent Russian and especially British expansion in the Middle East. U-boats entered the Persian Gulf, too close for comfort to His Imperial Majesty's oil interests at the delta town of Basra. And too close to India.

An expeditionary Force of the British Indian army under Major General Sir Charles Townshend was sent to capture Basra where, backed by the navy and meeting little opposition, it was victorious. Flushed with success, Townshend went on to conquer more Turkish territory and carried on towards Baghdad, 400 miles to the north.

He was not the first general to attempt to push his ill-equipped, tired men on to unachievable goals. Passing Kut, where he left some supplies, he got as far as Csetiphon, 16 miles south of Baghdad. He met unexpectedly strong resistance by the entrenched Turks. After many losses on both sides, he turned back to Kut and set about reinforcing his defences. As long as he held the town, the Turks had no way of advancing down river.

For the first six weeks the Turks tried to blast the British out of their stronghold by every means at their disposal, including an ancient brass cannon whose rumbling retort led the troops to call it 'Flatulent Flossie'. This tactic did not work but the situation changed when the February floods came. Stocks of food were ruined and sickness spread among the troops. At this point, a German military strategist, Field Marshal Baron van der Goltz, came onto the scene. Under his efficient command, the tired Turkish forces were spurred on to prevent relief parties from reaching Kut. The baron simply bided his time until the besieged garrison starved.

After 140 days and several unsuccessful attempts to relieve the siege, Townshend surrendered. Nine thousand surviving prisoners were marched across the desert to labour camps in Aleppo, many dying on the way; 250 villagers were publicly hanged by the Turks for having co-operated with the British.

Townshend is taken to Constantinople where he spends the rest of the war under house arrest.

In the meantime, Walter, in India, is undergoing two months of intensive training at Kirkee, drawing, tracing and acquiring the discipline needed to perfect his skills as a litho-draughtsman. He misses Joe's reassuring presence but he feels much more cheerful after an unexpected reminder of home.

Saturday, 2nd June 1917 (Kirkee Barracks)

Today I found an old paper 'The Vivio' dating back to Feb 20, 1915 & in it I saw 2 photos of some of my old chums in the 7th Devons. The photos were taken at Scarborough & were in the Daily Mirror about 2 years ago. It seems such a strange coincidence that I should find them in an old paper in India.

Emma has written 'answered' in her methodical hand-writing on the top left-hand corner of the next letter she receives from Walter.

'June 3rd, 1917

'My Dearest Mother,

'I was delighted to have your long loving letters of March & April. Joe forwarded them on to me, together with others from Ethel, Vera and "Tre". Also the photos of Percy, which are very nice, & such a nice sisterly letter to Joe and from Jeanne' (Jack's wife in Australia will prove to be a lifelong correspondent with Walter). 'I had not received mail for a long time, owing to being moved from place to place, so as you can guess, I was doubly glad to have such a bundle. I was very sorry indeed to hear that Mr Hindley is in the infirmary with leg trouble. Poor old fellow I would just love to see him and cheer him up a little. I sent him a letter by the mail last week c/o Mr Hankinson & I hope that he is better now.

'It was a surprise to read that Percy is already in France, but whatever he may have to go through I know he will make the best of it & I pray God that he will return to us safely. I am pleased to hear that dear Jim is quite well, give him my love when you write. I will write to him soon. I must also write to Percy & thank him for the photo.

'I received a letter from "Tre", only this time from hospital in Glasgow. Poor chap, he has had a very hard time, although he is always cheerful about things, & he has had many narrow escapes.

'Fortunately his trouble is slight, but I will quote his letter...

'"Well! You all, I have touched lucky at last, & I am back in dear old Blighty again. You remember I wrote to you from the Field Hospital. Well, I was sent out of there & again went into the trenches, but the poison was still in me, & consequently have a big abscess in the back, with which I was lucky enough to get sent back to England."

'Included with other experiences "Tre" went through before going to hospital is this one: "The night we went in it took us from 6 o'clock until 10 next morning to reach our post. Included in that is the fact that we found ourselves lost in the middle of the night & all went down into an old German dug out until dawn.

'"When I came out to go to hospital it was daylight. I could not get through the trenches by myself, for the thick mud, so accordingly I crawled out over the top. A

German sniper had four pots at me just when I was getting into a small wood which meant safety, but he missed each time."

'These are a few of the exciting times "Tre" has been in, & one can imagine how welcome a safe bed in Blighty must be.

'I hear from Joe that the 25ths are again on the move. It seems that they are moving further up, on to the N.W. Frontier, somewhere beyond the Indus River I think. Joe is quite well & I guess as big as ever, after spending those few weeks in the mountains.

'I am so glad that you enjoyed reading about the train journey I made to Burhan, although I am afraid that my letters have been somewhat smaller lately. Things have followed so fast and thick, that I have been at loss to connect up my diary.

'Today is the King's birthday, so we have a holiday.' (George V had come to the throne on the death of his father, Edward V11, in 1910.) 'It is now nearly 12.30, so that at home it will be about 7 o'clock, & I expect that you are just coming down to breakfast. Isn't it funny, just when you are having breakfast at 8 o'clock, we are having tiffin or dinner at 1.30 Indian time, you see we are five and a half hours ahead of London time, & when you are having tea, we are just turning in to bed.

'How is Billy? Has he been home on leave yet? Anyhow if that is a pleasure in store for him, tell him to leave some of the girls for his brother when he does arrive. I'm thinking he might squeeze 'em all to little bits, at least I know Joe & I shall when we come home, & you will have the biggest of them all, so I think I should warn you, so that you may have something to put out the fire handy.' (Sons and mothers in Victorian and Edwardian times had sentimental relationships that to us may seem embarrassingly sensual: Kaiser Wilhelm II couldn't wait to 'touch the insides of his mother's beautiful hands'.)

'When we were at Burhan we could not get a photo at all, & then our quick movements from place to place after leaving there made it impossible, however as soon as I am settled down here & have everything arranged I am going to have another photo taken at the works & the first one shall be for Vi.

'So pleased that Sue likes going to biz. I know I used to hate getting up at 5.00 am but Sue doesn't mind.

'Now I am going to "Bolo the bobagee" & shall tell him to "jelo" tiffin munkter on! Ek dum!" also "atora gurm char munkta geldee!" & after that I shall probably get my dinner & a cup of tea. So, making due apologies for the inner call, I will bring my letter to a close. My best love to Vidy & Sue & Joe & Rue,

'Your Loving Son, Wallie.

'PS My kind remembrances to the ladies who so kindly ask after us boys.'

Sunday, 17th June 1917

Went to Kirkee Church of Scotland this eve. A very nice service although the vicar is a bit of a rambler in his sermon. But then it is very pleasant & church in India has a distinct home viewpoint that appeals to me, as well as the worship therein.

Friday, 22nd June 1917

When Brown & I returned from office we were told that we were to go to new posts on Sunday.

'Tis very sudden & I hardly know how I shall be able to settle everything & write my letters. Tonight Brown, Cornwall, Reid & I had a fine supper at the Taj Hotel & a little time at the Napin Cinema.

Saturday, 23rd June 1917

This morning we went up to the works & received orders that we are to go to our new posts tomorrow. We have been busy drawing kits & signing various forms etc. Went into Poona to see Mr Audy but he was away. Had a pleasant night in Poona with Brown & Cornwall. I had my last supper at the Taj Hotel.

I was promoted to 2nd corporal today.

2nd Cpl. W E Barley
Royal Engineers
Sappers & Miners
Kirkee
India
June 23 1917

'My Dearest Mother,

'I have received more letters from Joe & with them came the sad news of poor Mr Hindley's death. I am so sorry, but perhaps it is for the best, & his end must have come as a happy release to one who had suffered much. Poor old fellow, he was always so cheerful. The evenings I had the good fortune to spend with him retain many pleasant memories. I wonder if you could get someone to place a bunch of roses on his grave for me? Poor Mr Hindley was fond of roses & I should like to have just a bunch of them for him & pay for them out of the money you have. Perhaps Mr Hankinson would do it?

'You see, I am now a corporal. I was promoted yesterday & my pay will be 12 annas per day extra, which is a considerable help. Today is Sunday and I have been very busy packing up my kit as I & another chap are going to Baghdad. We are leaving Kirkee tonight & I think we sail from Bombay on Monday. I am going as draughtsman & the other fellow as a litho printer. Anyway we shall have quite an easy time & all our work will be done at the Headqrs. in Baghdad, so you mustn't worry a wee bit. I have only just emerged from a pile of clothes, boots, kit etc. & I have yet to finish so can only make this a short note. We were only told on Friday night that we should be going so you can guess how we have had to rush about. I have just got my 'Sam Browne' belt & really I feel quite a soldier when I have got it on, it is so different to the heavy packs in ordinary equipment.'

This belt had a distinctive look with its attached strap going diagonally over the right shoulder to support holsters, pouches and first-aid kits etc. It was named after General Sir Samuel James Browne who wore one after losing an arm in battle. Walter was also issued with blue puttees which he wound neatly around his calves like crepe bandages and a sword which had a saw blade on one side. He secretly hoped its use would be ceremonial or for cutting through debris and undergrowth rather than attacking the Turks.

'Now dear Mother I must say tat-ta as my time is limited.

'My very best love to you dear & God bless you.

'Ever your loving Son, Wallie.

'PS Will you tell Mr Hankinson how sorry I am that I cannot write as promised but will do so as soon as I can. I told him I would write this week. Au Revoir Mother dear & here's a big kiss for you. Will write at first opportunity, although it may be a few weeks before it is possible. Am sending some things home as I thought they might be of use to Jim & Percy as I know wool is hard to get.

Sunday, 24th June 1917

Have been busily packing all the morning. I have had all manner of things to do now.

11.35pm: Have just entrained for Bombay. There are 2 sergeants & 2 cpls. besides ourselves & one native. We are all huddled up in a dirty third-class carriage but we were soon asleep. Tomorrow we shall be on the ship.

That summer is a not only a turning point for Walter; there are changes at home when the British Royal Family adopts the name Windsor and women over 30 get the vote. In the wider world, America's joining the war in April is beginning to take effect, with 10,000 US troops now in France. King Constantine 1 of Greece, a brother-in-law of Kaiser Wilhelm, abdicates in the face of Allied pressure and Ukraine proclaims independence from Russia.

In March, Kut Al Amara was taken by a new British force under the systematic General Sir Stanley Maude. In June he enters Baghdad, declaring 'Our armies do not come into your cities and lands as conquerors but as liberators.'

A huge amount of work awaits the liberators. Much of Mesopotamia has been devastated and its fragile infrastructure destroyed. Walter is to be part of the general's expeditionary force following him up the Tigris.

To reconstruct what has been lost, engineers are desperately needed and, in a land where there are no hills or horizons, so are mapmakers.

14

Heaven's Gate

*'Is it far, in regions old,
Where rivers flow o'er sands of gold?'
(The Better Land, Felicia Hemans)*

Monday, 25th June 1917

We arrived in Bombay at 6.20am and boarded the 'Multan' nine hours later. When the train steamed into the docks everything looked just as dirty as when I was here over a year ago. Our ship is a very small tramp steamer, & I can imagine that we shall have a rough journey. It is not very comfy & the deck space very limited. Left Bombay at midnight. Already fairly rough.

Tuesday, 26th June 1917

Ever since we left Bombay our ship has been ploughing through a heavy swell but today beats all & we have had an awful time with the boat rocking about, now rising to a huge swell, now dipping down to a trough & then up again. Often the waves break right over the decks & then they dip beneath the water & it is most difficult to move. I felt sick this morning.

Wednesday, 27th June 1817

Had a rotten night last night. The boat rolled so much from side to side that we slid first this way then that till our bones were aching sore. The sea is not quite as heavy today, have enjoyed some substantial meals although at present I can hardly write this, boat is pitching so much. We are about 30 hrs. off the gulf now.

Thursday, 28th June 1917

Today the ship has behaved very badly, pitching and plunging to a big swell, like some little cockle-boat. It is impossible to walk about or keep anything on the table.

It is also getting warm & we are gaining very little benefit from the voyage.

Friday 29th, June 1917

Today the sea is almost calm & we have passed numbers of fine large dolphins & schools of flying fish.

After skirting the southern coasts of India and Persia in such discomfort, not even the signs of land and the distant mountains of Oman excite Walter. The sea is much calmer once they round the Straits of Hormuz, which curve into the shelter of the Gulf of Persia above the sharp fingers of northern Oman, but there is worse to come.

This evening we sighted the Arabian coast on the leeward side of the ship. It was just a deep purple line, rugged & hilly, peeping up from the deep blue horizon. The heat is terrible. We are all without shirts & perspiration is running off us in streams.

Saturday, 30th June 1917

This morning the boat came to anchor a few miles off the Persian port of Bandar Abbas. We have been unloading cargo into a number of Turkish sailing vessels manned by Arabs.

The heat is awful, must be about 126 degrees (Fahrenheit) on deck. As I write this there is a pool of water on the table caused through perspiration & I feel like a pot of grease in a pair of underpants & no shirt.

This is just a taste of the discomfort Walter will have to endure in Mesopotamia. Extremes of temperature, desert storms, flooding, flies, mosquitoes and other vermin lead to appalling levels of sickness and death through disease.

Sunday, 1st July 1917

The temperature is a little better today owing to a fresh breeze from the N.E. We have lost sight of land & are sailing through calm seas.

Monday, 2nd July 1917

This afternoon we passed by the lightship & pilot vessels which stand out beyond the bar about 60 miles south of Shatt-al-Arab.

Could not go on tonight, tide is low so we have anchored outside the bar.

During the evening a hospital ship & six other large craft anchored alongside us.

Mesopotamia, 'the land between two rivers' was known as 'Mespot' to the advancing British. It did not change its name to Iraq until after World War I. The Euphrates and the Tigris meander through the length of the country for nearly 2,000 miles until they meet in the vast, marshy delta south of the bar where the *Multan* is now anchored. Shatt al-Arab, this dangerous place of shifting sands and sunken wrecks, is the gateway to the ancient 'cradle of civilisation': the home of early maps and the first form of writing, of the roots of Western philosophy and of theories embracing Judaism, Christianity and Islam.

It is also the source of myths and legends. The adventures of Sinbad the Sailor, one of Walter's favourite boyhood stories, have their origins here:

Sinbad sets off in search of adventure in the Persian Gulf. On the first of seven extraordinary voyages he reaches an island that suddenly disappears beneath the waves, taking all his unfortunate shipmates with it.

It turns out not to have been an island at all, but a gargantuan fish which has been floating there for so long that flotsam has accumulated on its back. Enticing paths led through rustling copses of reeds among its scales.

The story doesn't seem so far-fetched in this indefinable blend of land and sea where the waters from the giant rivers inexorably work their changes and nothing is constant.

Sinbad came home to Shatt-al-Arab with unimaginable riches. My father turned up with just his army issue kit, his diary and a few letters from home.

Tuesday, 3rd July 1917

We crossed the bar after brekkers this morning & after 3 hrs. run we sighted Shatt-al-Arab, its low-lying coastline made green by countless date palms.

Several fishing boats were out, looking quaint and picturesque. We passed boats sunk by the Turks to block the river, could see the funnels and masts of three ships.

Wednesday, 4th July 1917

Yesterday evening we arrived at Ashar Barracks. These are old Turkish barracks & consist of a high brick wall and outbuildings round a huge square. Since the British arrived huts have been built of reeds and mud, and water for washing and drinking has been laid on.

The Bks. are in the centre of Ashar & are used to house garrison troops & others on particular assignments from India. Expect to be here some time before we go on to Baghdad.

Walter has written extensive entries in his diary since leaving India, but so far no letters. He's keen to write home but paper is scarce and he's afraid his letters will be censored - as indeed they are. But he manages to get hold of some thin, lined paper and a letter to Emma, only part of which survives, vividly describes his experiences since leaving India.

Cpl. WE Barley,
Royal Engineers, "Litho Section"
G.H.Qrs. Mesopotamia. Ex. Force
July 4th, Basra

'My dearest Mother,

'The hot breath of the "Shamal" wind blowing across the great sandy veldt of the Arabian desert, the cries of many swarthy Arabs, as they pass down the little creek leading down the Tigris in their quaint narrow boats, & the sight of many date palms growing thickly by the waterside, tell me that I am really in Mesopotamia, although it seems but yesterday that I was in India.

'As a matter of fact our boat left Bombay on June 25th, & after a rough & not too pleasant voyage across the Indian Ocean we reached a part of the river where the small boats take over the passengers from the big "ships o' the sea", & bear them, day after day, up the long tedious stretch of water that lies between Basra & Baghdad. However we disembarked from our boat & came ashore, & now we are dumped down with many others in a large old barracks built by the Turks, but now in British hands...'

(The next page is missing. Perhaps Walter had overstepped the censor's mark.)

'...events as the day before, & although one passes places of historical interest, these are few & far between, & for the greater part it is glaring, scorching wilderness, from the edge of the river, to the horizon.'

This wilderness was not due just to natural erosion or damage from recent battles – it was also the result of much earlier war damage. In 1258 Hulagu, grandson of

Genghis Khan, invaded Mesopotamia. He and his Mongol hordes rampaged through the country, destroying the sophisticated irrigation system that had supported the entire area's civilization for hundreds of years. What was once an agricultural paradise became a steppe-like waste where only pastoral nomads could survive. Seven hundred years later, the conditions Walter describes are no easier.

'Here and there were the ruins of a once probably prosperous village. Sometimes we passed a few reed huts of wandering Arabs, from which a crowd of young women & naked boys, laden with pumpkins & eggs, would follow us along the river banks until we were sufficiently near for them to sell their goods. I have known instances when some of them have walked quite four miles along the river bank to sell a few eggs to us. It is really wonderful how the little Arab boys and girls can swim. The Tigris has a current or flow of six knots an hour, in spite of multitudinous bends and a great many whirlpools that tell of a treacherous undercurrent, yet these little urchins will plunge in ahead of the boat & swim downstream until they come level with us & then they cry out for buckshee & swim ashore with a biscuit or two that may be thrown to them.

'The bends & curves in the course of the river follow one another so quickly that sometimes we wonder if we are going up or down stream. Sometimes the river doubles back on its course so that at 4 o'clock one might be going west & at 4.30 going east. If there were an abundance of trees & grass one would easily imagine it to be the Norfolk Broads.

'The hot winds have been very strong & one gets so terribly thirsty.

'Oh those days were like the outlook: a repetition of sameness, for what could one do but read, drink & sleep, anything else was out of the question, for one felt too languid, & a military barge offers little convenience & little shelter from those burning winds.'

The Shamal starts in the Turkish hills and picks up dust from the desert and gets everywhere – into their hair, their clothes and even their food. Sometimes it blows a fine coating of dust as far as away as Bombay.

'How we looked forward to the coming of the evening & cool breezes. That mystic hour of desert afterglow, when everything is bathed in a wonderful crimson & green, the setting sun, when the silver crescent of the moon, & the brilliant evening star, shine like two beautiful jewels in the deep blue, just beyond the fast fading circle of sunlight. Then, as night draws a veil over all, one sees only the great black bar of desert land, & the star spangled heavens above. For a time the silence of the desert is broken only by the soft lapping of the waters about the boat, & an occasional discordant howl of a jackal, until suddenly, so suddenly that one might think at a given signal, the air vibrates with the whirring of myriads of ground insects, & it is not long before these pests have invaded every corner of the boat so that one is obliged to seek shelter beneath the mosquito net.

'And so the days & nights passed by until one evening we arrived at...'

(Walter is censoring himself, hardly necessary as his address in Basra is clearly shown at the top of his letter.)

'It was with feelings of great relief that I stepped ashore & made my way through dusty streets to G.H.Q.'

Having written to his mother from the 'large old barracks' built by the Turks, Walter continues his story in his diary.

Thursday, 5th July 1917

Walked through the bazaars this morning. These are all enclosed & very narrow. A large variety of goods may be obtained, including tobacco, and there are many Japanese & English general stores. The fruit shops are stocked chiefly with grapes, pumpkins & pomegranates. Tomatoes & dates are also plentiful.

On the whole the bazaars are cleaner than those in India and the smells are absent.

Friday, 6th July 1917

Paraded this morning @ 6am for quinine tablets.

Had charge of a party & worked until 7.30am. Good breakfast, bacon, bread & tea.

Lunch @ 1.15 bread & jam & tea. Dinner @ 5.15. roast meat & onions. The meat is Australian (frozen) & it was the best meal I have tasted since I left Blighty.

Temperature was 107 degrees in shade.

Two days after Walter writes from Basra, Emma puts pen to paper with encouraging words from Archibald Road.

Many letters between mother and son are written almost coincidentally, as though motivated by some shared sixth sense. Quite often they cross one another on the long journey between England and Mesopotamia.

6th July 1917

'My dearest Wallie,

'I am indeed glad and proud to know you have such a good chance to improve your position. I am sure, by your letters, you will be happy in your work, although I know how much you must miss that big-hearted brother Joe. It seems years now to me since you went away, but I am oh so thankful to God to know that up to now my Boys are safe & well. It has been a splendid experience for you and Joe & in later life it will bring many pleasant memories & smiles at the different things you had to do & put up with. I am, & so are you I know dear, glad that you tried hard once on a time to improve your drawing capabilities.

'Trying to educate oneself is time never wasted, & now you are just beginning to reap a little of your labour. I do hope when you come home you may be able to get into a good place, all here seem to think that it is a fine opportunity for you to improve your position & I think it will be your ambition to work for better things. We are all with you, good luck.'

While Emma continues with her correspondence in Archibald Road, Walter concentrates on conserving his energy as he toils up the Tigris in the heat. There is little to do aboard except watch the scenery and fill in his diary.

Saturday, 7th July 1917

Today the heat was very strong & have done nothing but drink lime juice. In the eve. went to palm gardens & had quite a pleasant time, sitting beneath the palms, sipping lemonade & listening to a native band playing snatches from Rag Times.

I shall be glad to get to Baghdad so I can get to work on something interesting.

Sunday, 8th July 1917

Issue of cigs & matches today. Have been trying to write letters but the heat makes me feel so drowsy, it is 118 degrees in the shade today & one doesn't feel like anything except lying down trying to keep cool.

I rather miss the church at Kirkee but one cannot expect too much on assignment -

indeed one must be thankful for small mercies.

The long stay in Basra anticipated by Walter only lasts a few days.

Monday, 9th July 1917

This morning I received instructions to pack up ready to move away this afternoon by 5.00pm. After packing we had inspection @ 10.30am. Stood in boiling sun half hour. Went to bazaar after dinner & got back 3.50. 4.15 parade then & marched to wharf. Sat about on the roadway until 10.30pm & then we were allowed to sleep on the pier for the night.

Tuesday, 10th July 1917

Embarked on barge this morning @ 5.00am. Waited about until 8.00am & then pushed out into mid-stream where we transferred ourselves & kit to a river steamer which is a big improvement. Again we waited in mid-stream until 5.15pm when we moved about 2 miles up-stream. Today has been a teaser &

almost dreary but one mustn't grumble especially as the boat is really decent.

Wednesday, 11th July 1917

This morning two barges were attached to either side of our boat, one is loaded with coal & the other is used by men from our boat. Continued pushing up-stream, passing always a long belt of date palms, which after a time grew monotonous with their sameness. Reached Al Qurnah & Garden of Eden about 3.00pm this afternoon just at the point where the Euphrates & Tigris Rivers meet. Qurnah is only a small place. The railway starts here & goes on to Amara. Awful heat today. Several are down with it.

Walter is too fed up with the heat to be enthusiastic about passing the Garden of Eden. This barren bit of semi-desert falls badly short of his expectations of the Gateway to Heaven, neither is it anything like Mrs Heman's *Better Land*. He would like to write home but finds it hard to be cheerful enough not to worry his mother – or the censor.

Arriving at a time when the water was low after the floods of the winter and early spring, there would have been nothing to see except muddy banks and dying vegetation. No apple trees, not a place where a serpent might lurk. Just a few dusty palms and scrubby bushes.

Even Walter's fertile imagination could not summon up a heavenly garden hidden behind the reeds, deep within the swamp where the magical floating islands of the Marsh Arabs were now beached in the mud.

He had arrived too late for the high waters when entire families and their animals passed the winter, Noah-like, on huge coracles formed of enormous dried reeds. These were waterproofed with the bitumen that bubbled out of the ground and had been used by the Marsh Arabs for centuries. On each island was a house, also made of reeds, arched over and cleverly woven into a small pillar at each corner. They made a fascinating sight when they were afloat but now, rotting and abandoned except for a few nomads, they added to the desolation of the area.

Thursday, 12th July 1917

Weather rather cooler now. Pass many more dwellings & the usual fruit & veg. sellers. Amazing how the young Arab ladies can swim.

Arrived at Amara. A really pretty place with dwellings dotted among trees. Eve, many lights shining along river. Quaint.

There is so much Walter wants to tell Emma but with paper still so scarce and censorship cramping his style, writing and sending letters home is harder than ever.

While Walter is moored at Amara, there are some fairly crisp questions in Parliament:

Hansard, 12th July, 1917

> **Mr King** asked the Secretary of State for India between what dates the soldiers in Mesopotamia were

prevented writing home except on printed post-cards specially supplied, and of which only a limited number were available?

Mr Macpherson: My right hon. Friend has asked me to answer this question. Since the date (16th February, 1916) on which the War Office assumed control, no such orders were issued.

Mr King asked the Under-Secretary of State for War (1) whether, having regard to the finding of the Mesopotamia Commission that the active intolerance of all criticism of defects or suggestions for reform had worked evils, he will say whether the field censorship on letters from the front is so exercised as to prevent friends at home knowing what soldiers are suffering or what might be improved; and whether he will state the principles on which censorship of letters from men on active service is enforced; and (2) whether the censorship is, or has been, used to prevent any complaints being sent to persons in this country as to the rationing of the troops abroad or the medical treatment of the sick and wounded.

Mr Macpherson: The principles are stated in Field Service Regulations, Part II Chap12, section 100 (6). Any complaint that those Regulations are being exercised in an unreasonable manner would form the subject of inquiry. No such complaints have been received, so far as I know.

Walter continues his narrative in his diary, where he is free to complain about his mosquito bites and the heat, hunger and tragedy aboard without fear of the censor's mark.

Saturday, 14th July 1917

The weather is even better to day and cooler. River is still very erratic with many twists & curves. Often the barges are driven on a mud bank causing delay. Have orange for lunch.

Sunday, 15th July 1917

Slept on board (cool) and was free from mosquitoes. These pests have simply covered my legs with red spots caused by their bites.

This afternoon the Shamal is blowing as if fanned from a hot oven. It is 122 degrees on boat.

Monday, 16th July 1917

We have progressed as far as Kut. The scene of many long struggles. The hot winds still prevail & the metal is so hot that one cannot touch it with bare hands. This heat makes one so terribly thirsty. We are 100 miles from Baghdad now, or 3 and a half days' journey. We may have a long stop here on account of a blockage on the river.

'The scene of many long struggles,' says Walter, making what happened on this loop in the river sound like history. Kut had been surrendered to the Turks only fifteen months previously, although the riverbank reveals little of its recent past. Dust has covered the damage of the winter floods. Nature, as relentless as war, continues to claim victims of its own.

Tuesday, 17th July 1917

Everyone was greatly alarmed yesterday eve when one of our chaps fell overboard. The strong current quickly bore the poor fellow downstream & before help could reach him, he had disappeared. I was washing on the barge at the time & had a shock when I saw the poor fellow swept swiftly past me only a few yards away.

Today we have only done 10 miles as we have been trying to refloat another boat off a mud-bank.

Wednesday, 18th July 1917

All day our boat has been trying to get the other boat off the bank. Two other boats came to our aid & eventually it was freed but only as evening was setting in. Of course we have hardly progressed at all & so another day is added to this long tiring journey.

Thursday, 19th July 1917

Making only slow progress upstream. The river still winds & doubles back in a most erratic way.

The system for getting water up on to the land is rather interesting & very like the principles of some Indian wells.

About 5.30 this evening we came up to where a barge lay almost dry on a bank & now we are trying to get it off. What a bother it is. Baghdad must still be a good many miles off.

Friday, 20th July 1917

Have suffered another loss on our boat. This morning a native fell overboard & disappeared instantly evidently sucked by strong undercurrents.

It is really very sad.

Have made better progress today but are still about 4 days journey from Baghdad & we are on half rations, bully beef & biscuits with porridge every other day.

Saturday, 21st July 1917

As we progress, on either side are ruined buildings, remains of once probably prosperous villages. The river is wide, almost 300 yds. across & as brown in colour as the sun-baked earth. It flows rapidly in spite of its multitudinous bends. The land is a flat bare wilderness relieved only by tufts of coarse grass & the decayed remains of habitation.

Sunday, 22nd July 1917

Today begins the 11th day of our travels on this boat.

We are still passing the dreary flat stretches of barren land, now too familiar a sight. The hot winds blow straight at us with merciless fury so that one would think the very gates of Hades were opening on to us. It is awful. The metal gets too hot for one's hand to bear & our throats get very dry. Frequent cases of heat stroke.

The evenings are much to be thankful for. The cool breezes and exquisite sunsets seem to drive away all oppression endured by day.

Monday, 23th July 1917

We have endured yet another loss through drowning. The poor chap was climbing from a motor-boat on to ours, when a slip sent him heading into the boiling current of the treacherous river & in a few moments he was lost to sight. Ours is truly an unfortunate boat.

To relieve the stress of the journey, Walter has been reading *Thaïs*, Anatole France's novel about the path to redemption of the most beautiful courtesan in Egypt and a libertine monk from the desert.

I think it a fine description of the old Christian era & of the lives & speech of those wild fanatic men who lived outside the boundaries of those great cities where wine ran free in the blood of pleasure-loving courtesans.

Tuesday, 24th July 1917

All day we have been watching the horizon for the roofs of Baghdad, but not until sunset were we rewarded by seeing, here and there *amid groves of palms, the pretty houses of the well-to-do Arabs.*

At last we pulled into a jetty and disembarked. We then marched or rather stumbled to a rest camp, loaded with every stitch of our kit.

Slept out in open tonight, but expect we shall be sent on to G.H.Q. tomorrow.

Wednesday, 25th July 1917

Rose at 6.00am & boarded a swift little tug at 8 o'clock which took us up river to H.Q. where we got 2 coolies to carry our kit. After asking our direction several times we finally arrived at Litho Section, an impressive building which will also be our billet.

I am thankful our journey is ended.

15

Eighty Days in Baghdad

The day after his arrival, Walter gets down to work. There's no spare time for writing letters but he continues to keep his diary up to date.

Thursday, 26th July 1917

Have been helping with some maps of Baghdad which are being coloured. Have not yet seen Major Gunter who I hear is a very stern & strict man.

The work here is really 1st class & most of the fellows have been years at their travails.

Friday, 27th July 1917

We have a fine Indian bobajee to cook for us. The mess pays him 5 rupees per man per month, & we get very good attention & a full menu in return. Really to come back to a three-course dinner at 7 o'clock in the evening is fine.

Walter is working with an elite group of map-makers and using some of the most up-to-date equipment available at the time, thanks largely to a visit to Mesopotamia in 1916 by Lawrence of Arabia. He had proposed that maps of Turkish trenches should be compiled from aerial photographs, following a system which had already been used in Gallipoli and Sinai. A Map Compilation Section had duly been established at G.H.Q with the latest photographic equipment.

Saturday, 28th July 1917

This morning as a test I had to draw freehand a list of navigation symbols used on the R. Tigris. Went out into the narrow courts of the city this afternoon & got one or two little sketches.

Sunday, 29th July 1917

Have nearly finished my test & have only a few lines to add. I am not feeling too well, having caught a chill to my stomach.

We all sleep on the roofs here. From our roof we look over the city & it is so strange to see people going to bed all around & look at the minarets & domes of the mosque peeping up in the night sky.

At last Walter has time to write home – unfortunately from a hospital bed. The 'chill to his stomach' turns out to be dysentery. He tells Emma nothing of this in his next letter home.

2nd Cpl. W.E. Barley,
Photo Litho Section,
G.H.Qrs. M.E.7
30th July

'My Dearest Mother

'At last, after 3 long weeks I am able to write to you. Since I wrote from ...' (again, the stern hand of the censor). 'We have travelled for many days up the winding course of the Tigris and now I am writing from THE place & relieved by the thought that I am at my journey's end at last.

'When we arrived at our billet, which was once a large house, we entered a small square courtyard through a large wooden door. From this courtyard a low passage leads into a large square with a fountain at its centre, the spray playing gently on the green boughs of the orange trees surrounding it. A large verandah overhangs the court.

'The buildings are quite Eastern in effect, being painted in a mosaic fashion, blue, brown, yellow and white. These are our offices & most comfortable & large rooms they are. Following a low passage and a long corridor you come to a bright room where I & seven other fellows live. We pass from this room, along another corridor at the end of which is a narrow staircase leading up onto the roof. Here you will see our beds all neatly arranged in two rows & if you just look over the wall you can see many other roof bedrooms, whilst above all rise the minarets & domes of many mosques.

'NOW Mother dear I am just waiting to hear from you. Your letters will be on the way to me, but of course I have not received any since I left India although I am hoping for a big batch soon. How are you all? & are Jim & Percy still A.1. & have you heard from Billy & how are you dear? Well I must be busy with letters now after this long delay. I often think of Daisy and Bert. I hope Bert is quite well & has he had any exciting times?

'WELL I must write to Daisy for I should so much like to have a letter from her. Then there is Lily too, I really think I ought to put a little gunpowder in my letter to her.

'Please give my best love to all the dear girls & boys. With very much love & a big kiss for you dear.

'Yr. loving Son, Wallie

'P.S. Since leaving Jullunder I have travelled about 5,000 miles.'

Walter seems to be quite cheerful when he writes his letter to Emma. But the following diary entry, written in pencil on the same day, tells a different story.

Monday, 30th July 1917

Have been admitted into hospital today with trouble in my tummy, what a jolly nuisance it is. I have so much to do & I want to write my letters but of course I haven't a scrap of paper or pen.

I am having milk with Horlicks milk & tea.

Tuesday 31st July 1917

I am fairly much the same today & very hungry.

I was conveyed to the 23rd Bttln. Gen. Hospital this evening. This hospital is a fine large building being fitted with electric lights & fans & having a total of ...'

Walter mentions later that his ward contains 42 beds, but here, still wary of the censor, he misses out the total.

The grounds are very pleasant. The hospital was taken from the Turks when we captured Baghdad.

A thousand years before Walter travelled up the Tigris, Baghdad was at its cultural peak. There were great libraries, schools of philosophy where the works of Aristotle were studied, and a fine hospital with separate wards for men and women. So skilled were its medical practitioners that their teachings were followed in Europe for hundreds of years.

The hospital's location had been chosen carefully. Pieces of meat were hung in places that seemed most suitable and allowed to rot. It was built on the site where the meat stayed fresher longer, where the air was clean and the 24 specialist doctors could attend to their patients in perfect conditions.

The great building was appointed like a palace and supplied with plentiful water from the Tigris and medicinal herbs from its own gardens.

Patients, princes and paupers alike, were comforted by music and story-telling; when they left they were given gold pieces to contribute towards their convalescence.

All this had come to an end when Hulagu Khan, having obliterated access to Mesopotamia's most valuable resource, its water, set out to destroy its intellectual and cultural life by sacking Baghdad to avenge the death of a brother. *'When I lead my army against Baghdad in anger, whether you hide in heaven or in earth, I will bring you down from the spinning spheres; like a lion, I will toss you in the air. I will leave no one alive in your realm; I will burn your city, your land, your self.'*

He made a pyramid of the skulls of its scholars, religious leaders and poets. Two hundred years later it was the turn of Tamerlane the Great to sweep down to Baghdad. Once more intellectuals were murdered, hospitals destroyed and libraries burned. It was said that the ink of countless medical and scientific works ran into the bloodstained waters of the Tigris.

The bright flame of civilization was extinguished and Mesopotamia became a neglected frontier province ruled from the Mongol capital of Tabriz in what is now Iran. Only a residual glow of its knowledge remained in the folklore of the tribes inhabiting the marshlands and desert valleys of this former Garden of Eden.

Some of Baghdad's great institutions, including its hospital, were rebuilt under the Ottomans by Suleyman the Magnificent. From 1534 until his death in 1566 Mesopotamia thrived once more, but the cycle of destruction went on as access to food, political power and religious domination became as contentious as territory.

By the time General Maude walked into Baghdad it had once more been decimated by war although the 'new' hospital survived. When Walter was taken in four months later, it was up and running, staffed by British doctors and nurses. He was not too ill to appreciate the 'fine building' and its modern amenities.

But there was to be no music or story-telling for Walter and his fellow patients. Just the moans of the sick, the whirr of fans and clatter of nurses moving iron bedsteads and rattling in with trolleys.

Wednesday, 1st August, 1917

I am put on No Diet. Have a touch of dysentery.

Dysentery was, and still is, a debilitating and sometimes fatal disease. The effects are similar to gastroenteritis, commonly caused by the shigella virus rather than E. coli or salmonella, and characterised by knife-like pain and liquid diarrhoea, often with blood and mucus. It normally takes its course without special treatment. Rehydration and resumption of a gentle diet usually work after a few days but it leaves the patient weak and completely drained of energy. Today Walter would probably have been fed on bananas, rice and apple sauce, but at the time malted milk served its purpose.

The benign conditions under which he was treated bear no comparison to the hellish circumstances earlier in the Mesopotamia campaign. The following is part of a report by Major R M Carter of the Indian Medical Service who watched a river steamer bringing the wounded into Basra in 1915:

'I was standing on the bridge in the evening when the 'Medjidieh' arrived. She had two steel barges, without any protection against the rain, as far as I remember. As this ship came up to us I saw that she was absolutely packed, and the barges too, with men. When she was about 300 or 400 yards off it looked as if she was festooned with ropes. The barges were slipped, and the 'Medjidieh' was brought alongside the Varela. The stench when she was close was quite definite.'

The major was horrified to find that 'What I mistook for ropes were dried stalactites of human faeces. The patients were so huddled and crowded together on the ship that they could not perform the offices of nature clear of the edge of the ship...'

As well as sickness, the men had had to endure rain and extreme temperatures with little or no shelter or fresh food. Carter expected very few of them to survive.

He was accused of being a trifling busybody by the establishment at the Indian Medical Service. However he was eventually promoted to Lieutenant-General and several of his suggestions, such as the installation of electric fans, had been implemented when Walter was admitted to the hospital.

Thursday, 2nd August 1917

No Diet.

Walter is still in hospital for the third anniversary of the declaration of War on 6th August 1914. All he could think of then was joining the army and fighting for his country. Now, three years later, as he lies on his hospital bed, he looks back from a different perspective. He's still patriotic and is proud of the work he has done with his maps. But nothing can make up for the anguish he feels at so much loss of life.

Monday, 13th August 1917

Much better today. I am now allowed a portion of fish & a custard at midday. This mail has brought no letters for me. I am waiting anxiously for news from Joe. I hear the battalion has done very good work on the frontier.

Bravo Londons.

Brother Joe was still in India with the 25th London Regiment. Walter is referring to the quelling of an uprising by the Wazristani tribesmen on what is now the border with Pakistan and Afghanistan.

Wednesday, 15th August 1917

Klute, a friend from my old battalion, came to see me this evening. He brought 3 Christian Lifes but no letters.

I hear that the Londons have had 300 casualties including sick. These are heavy losses but sickness has taken a big toll & I am anxiously waiting news from Joe.

The Londons have been mentioned in despatches. Bravo Londons good luck to you all.

Thursday, 16th August 1917

I have been making some cards for the sister in the Lower Ward. I have to make 42 & number them from 1 – upwards, 42 being number of beds in this ward.

Monday, 20th August 1917

I left hospital today, thank goodness. I am feeling much better but weak. Hired a boat to take me & kit down to billets. The days of enforced idleness do get on one's nerves, although one gets every attention & comfort at the hospital & the sisters are quite nice.

Only 'quite nice'? After spending so long seeing no-one but weary or wounded soldiers, the nurses in their clean, crisp uniforms and starched white head-dresses, like the wings of administering angels, would surely have overwhelmed Walter? But, like many young men of his generation, he kept his innermost thoughts to himself where women were concerned.

The harassed nurses themselves had little time for social chit-chat with this rather gaunt young man who made jokes and did amusing drawings. They'd left their families and lives of comfortable predictability for the excitement of the battle-front. Reality had toughened them. Their bravery and glamour made them heroines in the eyes of the young women left behind, and little girls like Walter's nieces who dressed themselves up to look like small Florence Nightingales.

Violet, the most willing and put-upon of Walter's older sisters, would also have loved being a nurse, looking after wounded soldiers in France, India or Mesopotamia. But poor 'Vidy' was stuck in London, making munitions at the Arsenal. Handling explosives was dangerous work and accidents were common, but Violet would always be an unsung heroine, trudging stoically back and forth to Archibald Road in the evenings to look after her parents. Emma's legs were beginning to cause problems and James was drinking heavily. She was needed, if not cherished.

Tuesday, 21st August 1917

Quite good to be back with the boys again, but I do not think I shall be here long as Q.M. Henley says I shall be going to 3rd Army Camp. H.Q. which if true will be rotten, as Taylor & Klute are both from my old Batt. & like all the boys here are very nice fellows.

Thursday, 23rd August 1917

I have done a map today & I felt better.
I am to go to 32nd A.C. tonight. I wonder when I shall be able to settle down? Left G.H.Q this eve. & went sailing down the streets with three boys to carry my baggage & charpoy.

3.A.C. is much smaller than G.H.Q & does not do half the work. I am sorry, as at this point I should like to do all I can to help with my future work.

Friday, 24th August 1917

Still no mail. I am wondering what has happened to the letters & if old Joe has *forwarded them, but I suppose they will come soon. I hope so. I feel like someone on a desert island. I now realise what a great blessing the letters are that bear to us the news of the dear folks at home.*

Saturday, 25th August 1917

No 5 (8) Litho & No 2 Brushing Sections work together in two half-basement rooms in a big Arab house used as 3rd Corps H.Q. It is situated on the river bank & almost next door to Gen. Maude's residence & the U.S.A. consulate. We have a Regular Army G (Q) M.S in charge, then Lieut. Chappel & Klute & me & five or six natives.

Sunday, 26th August 1917

Rex Smith & I went to the evening service at G.H.Q.

This is the first mention of Rex Smith who is to become a lifelong friend.

It is held in a small room with a plain altar & a tiny harmonium & the congregation were in number about ten officers & twenty men. Curiously enough, the padre was a fellow who used to take the services for the 25th at Hebbel Camp in Bangalore.

Sunday, 2nd September 1917

Went to church at G.H.Q. I rather enjoy these services which are quite simple & more to my liking than some of the Church of England services.

Monday, 10th September 1917

Left for hospital with return of old complaint. Just before leaving I had three letters from Mabs & one from Mr Hankinson & one from Vera. I am so glad to have news from home & coming just now I feel very cheered.

The following flowery letter from Walter's sister Mabs is the only one of these three letters to survive. Although it took more than four months to reach him it arrived at just the right time to shower him with much needed affection in this parched period of his existence. Clever, authoritative Mabel had her mother's energy and streak of sentimentality. She was very fond of her younger brother.

The Cottage,
Chipperfield, Herts
May 4. 1917

'Now Wally dear my thoughts are all for you for a while, & I have to stop writing just a minute as it seems as if you were at my side, I can hear your voice – you know the gruff tone you've got now since you're a man – & I see the gleaming twinkle in your dear eyes as we talk to each other. I imagine sometimes when you are thinking home thoughts you must feel a flood of happiness come to you for all the loving thoughts that we send towards you. It is such a wonderful thing to feel loved & though we all loved each other before you went away – you never were more loved than now.

'We feel I think the strength of the bond that unites us all, so much more for this absence, & it has shewn too what deep sympathy there is between us all. Sometimes, when I'm quiet & alone, you don't seem at all far away. The power of thought is mighty & who knows perhaps your thoughts & mine may meet somewhere in the silent ways that lead from one to the other of us & draw us very near.

'I hope you have not had too hard & strenuous a time; I wish I could sometimes do some of your work for you when you are tired, or give you nice cooling drinks when you are hot & thirsty – pop out like a fairy with a jug as long as your arm, full of iced fruit drink – Poor darlings you have all to go through it & I seem to do so little for you.

'I wish you were here to enjoy the beauty & peace of the country spread all around me. The trees are most lovely – the cherry trees are laden with snowy blossom, the hedgerows are so dainty and green & the sun shines so soft & warm from the blue sky – just over my head a biplane is whirring as it rapidly passes.

'The garden begins to look so lovely now – everything is very late, but we have had a fortnight of perfectly lovely sunshiny weather – quite hot enough for summer & that has helped things wonderfully.

'Marjorie has just returned to school. We went to stay with Granny for a night before she went back & all took a jaunt to the theatre in the evening. It cheered Mother up a bit & she enjoyed it in spite of her difficulty in getting along but Nicky is a good prop & we had a very happy time.'

Bill Nicholas, Mabel's second husband, was by all accounts urbane, wealthy and benevolent. He paid for Marjorie's school fees at an exclusive boarding school in Eastbourne. Mabel had worked as a hotel receptionist after her divorce and this was how she met 'Nicky'.

'I should love you to see the garden. The tulips of perfect colouring, rose, purple, pearl pink & bright crimson – many sorts of daffodils, Golden Spur, & a bi-colour variety of two yellows & a simple yellow with a deep orange eye – & those beautiful white pheasant-eyed narcissi. The hyacinths are late – but the forget-me-not borders to my wally-wallflowers are growing well & the polyanthus border is full of every variety of colour – so are the violas & pansies – they're extra splendid. My herbacious border is going to be wonderful this year & I am looking forward eagerly to its perfection.

'How very kind of Miss Barmby's friend to send you *Punch* so regularly. But there, dear old thing, how kind all your Devon friends were & are – how I hope to meet some of them with you one day & how I picture the times we're to have over the moors together.

'I am sending Percy a parcel which I have to pack & do up to catch post so (if it won't spoil your moustache) I am giving you a big kiss to say goodbye with for a little while. I shall write again soon dear boy.

'God keep you – with dear love from your loving sister, Mabs.

'PS Thanks for No. 4 Londoner! In haste.

'Footnote – No 5 Londoner has just come in as am posting this.'

Tuesday, 11th September 1917

Am feeling well & quite hungry, a good sign. The fellow in the next bed to me, Cpl. Pollard, is a nice chap, hailing from Westminster. We have some jolly talks together about our various experiences, so that the time passes quite pleasantly. He is in the RAMC (Royal Army Medical Corps) & has worked on motor ambulances out here for some time.

Sunday, 16th September 1917

Left hospital today, feeling much better. Went round to G.H.Q. on way back to see all the boys. On my arrival at 3rd Corp I was greeted with a little batch of letters. I am just as happy as can be.

It is jolly to have news & there are some lovely letters from Mother & Mabs.

Monday, 17th September 1917

Have been out for my usual walk along the banks of the Tigris. The mornings are really lovely now, with the cool fresh breezes blowing & the sun shining brightly but without the awful heat it usually brings later in the day.

Tuesday, 18th September 1917

We have experienced a sudden cold spell. The nights on the roof are very cold indeed & one needs 2 blankets as well as overcoat for covering.

The mornings are usually delightful & I enjoy my little walks very much.

Wednesday, 19th September 1917

I am feeling much better than I have for many weeks.

Friday, 21st September 1917

Went for a long walk through the Arab quarter of Baghdad this morning & nearly lost myself in a maze of small courtyards. Finally emerged into an Arab bazaar from where I soon found my way back through the narrow streets.

The atmosphere of these narrow streets is evoked by Percival London, a correspondent of the *Daily Telegraph*. He is fascinated by the city's past but you can almost see him shudder at the sight of so much evidence of Europe's mass-production:

Of all cities and towns beneath the sun there is none like Baghdad for the associations of light and colour, luxury, romance and blood that the very name conjures up. Yet she is for the most part a raffle of houses of sun-burned mud and evil-smelling alleys, with scarcely a building shouldering its way into prominence above the jostle of flat and dirty roofs below.

The romance of Bagdad does not lie on the surface. A little may still be found in the closed-in bazaar, with its long vistas barred by slanting beams of blue sunlight, and the small shops – little alcoves in which the semi-darkness partly conceals that totally shameless Europeanisation of just about everything exposed for sale.

The brand of Manchester or of Germany is in almost every strip of stuff. Even if you ask for the coarse black hop-sack-like cloth of which the Arabs make their abba, or outer cloak, you will have it brought to you with a shiny black label on the wrapper explaining in gold letters, quite incomprehensible both to buyer and seller, that it is of extra quality, and that it comes from England, beside the Ship Canal or the Aire.

But if one can turn one's eyes from our glazed chintzes and terrible velveteens, from the lamps with coloured globes made in Austria, and from the gay and flimsy metal work of Germany, there is much the same scene in the bazaar as in the days of Caliph Haroun-el-Raschid: the laden donkeys butt and barge their way through, the Arab in from the desert moves with a fine, slow step among the town-keeping trash; a melon and orange stall is loaded like a heap of gargantuan emeralds and fine opals where the blue ray strikes it from the roof; veiled women plod by in couples, and the naked black-eyed children tumble and squall at their feet.

One wonders if there ever was invented so beautiful a head-dress as the chifeyeb and the binding cord of the agal: and why the entire world does not wear red shoes.

The clinking saucers of the sherbet seller are attractive until one recalls the high death-rate of the town.

The Kavé-khanas will give you the best Turkish coffee to be had outside the Red Sea littoral.

All is both commotion and quiet.

(Percival London, the Daily Telegraph 1915.)

Saturday, 22nd September 1917

I had another batch of letters today from Joe. It was so nice to read home news especially on this my birthday.

Sunday, 30th September 1917

Good news has reached us from up line. The 15th Division who only left Baghdad a few days ago were in action yesterday and captured about 4,000 prisoners & a few guns. Also Gen. Ahmed Bey, who took Gen. Townshend prisoner at Kut. This is good news indeed & a feather in the cap of the 15th who have not until now been in action.

Monday, 1st October 1917

Sent money order for £2.10s.0d to mother, also order for 25 rupees to JK Harker & Co. for paints etc.

Thursday, 4th October 1917

A large number of Turkish prisoners marched through Baghdad today. About 600 all told. They looked very sunburnt & were dressed in all kinds of stuff, mostly rags. All ages & sizes & a few Arabs.

Thursday, 11th October 1917

Hustle & bustle everywhere today. Packing up in readiness to move away.

The Printing Section leaves us with all the baggage carts. Tomorrow morning we shall go up river via motor-boat to board the train.

Saturday, 13th October 1917

Left Baghdad with remainder of 3rd Corps. We were all bundled onto a train full of high explosives.

Walter takes this journey very calmly. Transporting a load of high explosives across the desert on railway lines distorted by war and weather would have been dangerous enough. With troops on board it was courting disaster.

16

Dogs of War and other Mercenaries

The train arrived safely at Baqubah, in spite of the bad condition of the railway lines, the nature of its cargo and the ever-present danger of ambush. The explosives were intended to prevent Turkish forces, entrenched at various points north of Baghdad, from returning to the city.

General Maude himself advanced no further but he dispatched several forces up-river to undertake the task. This was successfully accomplished at great cost to his own army – 40,000 of his men died, more of them from heat-stroke and disease than in battle.

With Baqubah secure, the British could begin reparations in the area, and Walter could get on with a new set of maps.

Daily life is relaxed and almost luxurious, as he notes in his diary: 'The camp is situated amid pleasant surroundings and far exceeds expectations.'

On his time off, he strolls through plantations of palms, picks the fruit from pomegranate and orange trees and enjoys the informality of sleeping under canvas once more: 'We have plenty of room, an EP tent for work, a 160-pounder mess tent for meals & our own bell tent.'

Tuesday, 16th October 1917

This morning we went to buy eggs from a little village on banks of the canal half a mile south of camp. However could not get more than 9 for a rupee whereas we were normally sold 24 for a rupee. Somebody should wake these Arabs up a bit. Walked through the village this evening, very interesting & pretty.

By now Walter has become firm friends with Rex Smith and has acquired another, smaller chum, a little dog he calls Jim, who provides some of the companionship he has missed so much since leaving India.

This Mesopotamian mutt just turns up one day in Walter's correspondence, as he probably did in real life. He may have been left behind by a soldier passing through the camp earlier on, or been wandering hungrily around one of the scruffy villages hoping someone would adopt him.

Dogs had been part of Mesopotamian culture for thousands of years. A protective figurine discovered in the foundation of an ancient building bears the inscription, 'Don't stop to Think. Bite!' Dogs were also associated with the goddess of healing, perhaps because ancient physicians noted that wounds licked by dogs healed better.

On the Western front they were playing a vital part as messengers between the trenches - faster than humans, smaller targets for snipers and very reliable as long as they were well trained. Deaths were not infrequent but desertion was rare. Like Jim, they were loyal companions.

Now that the awful conditions he had endured travelling up the Tigris are behind him, Walter's enthusiasm returns. There are new sights, sounds and smells to describe to Emma.

'After an early breakfast, two chums & I went out for a walk, with my dog Jim chasing on ahead full of fun. Our path led by a narrow canal, the banks of which were mud walls with clumps of date palms topping over them & occasionally quaint old houses of the Arabs with the usual complement of kiddies, chickens, donkeys, dirt, & snarling dogs, & of course smells.

'Presently we came into the town of Baqubah, where we spent an interesting hour picking our way down the tiny narrow streets, looking in at open doors of houses leading into the inner yards, where sometimes we saw groups of women folk, dressed in dirty black & brown clothes that covered them from head to heel, seated round open fires, & sometimes a heap of dirty children playing together, whilst at times we saw just an empty yard, with all its queer dark corners & earthenware pots & a worn earth stairway leading up to the rooms on the floor above.

'And so we walked on until we came into the old bazaar, dark & dirty, with half its roof-covering rotted and fallen away & a queer jumble of shops beneath, looking more like cellars than anything, except where stacks of oranges were piled up for sale, or where little furnaces in the tinkers' shops lit up the darkness & the swarthy faces of Arab men at work. Here & there we passed through the cafés, so called for want of a name, but which were merely a jumble of rough wooden benches set close together in a dark open space in the bazaar upon which the Arabs sit & puff at cigarettes & munch great pieces of flat round chapatas, procured from a boy who sits over a slow charcoal fire & cooks these pancake-like edibles on a sheet of iron.

'Having passed through the town, we came upon a pretty lane, bounded on either side by high mud walls dividing the fruit gardens, & over which trailed many blackberry brambles & above them the dark green foliage & the golden fruit of the orange hung temptingly whilst high above all waved the tall top-knots of the palms.

'Entering the lane, we presently came to where the pathway sloped down to the River Diyalah. Here the lane ended, & on the other side of the river one could see only the bare grey banks & beyond them the barren desolation of the desert.

'A gap in one of the walls led into the fruit gardens & on entering we looked upon a lovely scene. High above us the green fronds of the palms swayed & rustled against the blue, flecked sky, whilst below & around us, a riot of gold & green of numerous orange trees, loaded down by a glorious wealth of fruit, with here & there a pomegranate tree, just now resplendent in Autumn's cloak of amber, whilst underfoot the earth was carpeted a delicate shade of green from a clover-like plant.

'Walking amid this glorious setting, we espied a little path which we followed, bending now & then to avoid the clusters of low hanging oranges, until we came upon two mat huts, surrounded by dense foliage & evidently the night quarters of the keepers for, in the far corners, were bundles of rags made into blankets & used no doubt as beds. In the centre of the huts were the remains of charcoal fires.

'However as we could see no one about we continued on down the path, picking now & then the choicest of the fruit as we went along.

'All this time my dog had been enjoying himself immensely, chasing all sorts of imaginary animals & scraping up suspicious looking holes in the earth & rushing off with a twig in his mouth. Suddenly he pricked up his ears & growled out a challenge to a big brown dog that had made an appearance through a thicket near by. However, seeing four of us the dog contented itself by barking furiously & followed us at a respectable distance. At last, when we had come to the further end of the orchard, our pockets & handkerchiefs filled with golden fruit, we clambered over the wall and descended onto a little riverside pathway, along which we made our way back to camp.

'And now just a word about my little dog.

'Jim is a fine little animal & a cheerful comrade, always eager to play & a very brave little chap. He always accompanies me on my walks & has no fear of the big snarling pariah dogs that always hang around the villages & are vicious half wild types of cur. I have known my little dog to stand up against two great dogs who came for him when we were out walking, & Jim put up such a display of bared teeth & ferocious growls that they merely stood still & let him pass by, not daring to come near him.

'At night he sleeps in a little box of straw at the foot of my bed, where he remains, fairly quiet, until morning, when our tea is brought in by our boy, an Indian by the name of Lal Lu!'

Away from the fertile river banks where the British troops lived in relative comfort, the desolation of the desert stretched as far as the eye could see. The vanquished and the dispossessed, many of them mercenaries from both sides, struggled to survive.

Wednesday, 17th October 1917

A few Turks brought in today. They seem in good condition but very dirty and ragged. Often our police bring straggling Arabs & Indians into camp where they have to give account of themselves.

Many of the Indian soldiers brought into camp would have been mercenaries, mostly Mohammedan, recruited from the barren plains north of Bombay. Walter does not say what side these men were fighting for, but desertion from the British forces was rare, in spite of the fatwa issued by the Ottomans at the beginning of the war. Even if they had seen the proclamation, most of them were illiterate so it would have meant nothing to them.

Thursday, 18th October 1917

The weather is much improved. Days are cooler, growing colder as night comes on.

Clouds hanging above today, Cull & I have dug down 1 foot into tent floor & entrenched about the tent outside for fear of showers.

This was wise; autumn 'showers' in the Tigris/Euphrates plain came down in deluges.

Saturday, 20th October 1917

Two of the interpreters brought four Armenians into camp this evening. The poor chaps were in an awful state. They had been wandering about feeding on grass, working for Arabs and existing on anything they could find for a number of months. Their clothes were in rags.

These starving men could have been some of the few survivors of the Turkish genocide which had decimated a huge proportion of the Armenian population in 1915.

Armenia is a tiny, inland country – about the size of Ireland – caught between the Caspian and Black Seas. Much of its population had, over centuries, emigrated to neighbouring countries whose armies they had joined in times of war, but mostly they just got on with their lives, worshipping in their ornate churches whose form of Christianity dated back over a thousand years. Their choirs sang the hymns of their forefathers in bass voices that reached the very depths of the soul.

With the repressive 'Turkification' of the old Ottoman empire came the rumblings of Armenian nationalism, violently repressed after generations of tolerance by the Turkish community.

Those who could had fled to neighbouring countries, including Syria. The following letter, written earlier in the month by four members of a German mission in Aleppo to the Imperial German Ministry of Foreign affairs in Berlin, is a sad reflection on the attitude of Germany's ruler twenty years later:

> *'We think it our duty to draw the attention of the Ministry of Foreign Affairs to the fact that our school work will be deprived of its moral basis and will lose all authority in the eyes of the local population if it is really beyond the power of the German Government to mitigate the brutality of the treatment which the exiled women and children of the massacred Armenians are receiving.*

'In the face of the scenes of horror which are being unfolded daily before our eyes in the neighbourhood of our school, our educational activity becomes a mockery of humanity. How can we make our pupils listen to the Tales of the Seven Dwarfs, how can we teach them conjugations and declensions when, in the compounds next door, death is carrying off their starving compatriots, when there are girls and women and children, practically naked, some lying on the ground, others stretched between the dead or the coffins made ready for them beforehand, and breathing their last breath.'

Hitler, planning to invade Poland in WW2, is supposed to have said, 'Who now remembers the Armenians?'

A later conflict in 1918, between Armenia and Azerbajan – again different in culture, religion and ethnicity, has an up-to-date connection with Walter's grandson, David Barley. On a solo motorbike expedition through Turkey, Azerbajan and Uzbekistan en route to Vladivostok in 2010, he found they were still at each other's throats. 'The Armenians,' he wrote, 'The Azeris hate them!' Crossing the Caspian Sea, his ferry was stuck offshore for a few days. On board was a huge and scary Azeri army recruitment officer who had been in prison. He befriended David and as a token of his goodwill promised to kill any Armenian who gave him trouble.

Tuesday, 23rd October 1917

One of the fellows down with fever only slight I think.

Saturday, 3rd November 1917

After working hours Rex & I went for a swim in the Diyala. A keen nip in the water made us feel all aglow. The dogs were with us and they also had a swim & afterwards rolled over the shelving bank like mad things. Good appetite, good drinks, bed.

Sunday, 4th November 1917

Went for usual walk across desert where we watched a splendid sunset. Right on the horizon a bar of deep green, above which flaming red clouds stretched across the sky, & bright pale blue above the red gold, fading into deep blue rings splashed with red clouds. Went to kirk this evening.

Tuesday, 6th November 1917

No Parade for physical this morning, but had game of footer instead.

Friday, 9th November 1917

An aeroplane scare this morning, but further than the warning, nothing happened.

Busy on secret map of defences.

Saturday, 10th November 1917

More Turkish deserters arrived here from up line today, including an officer. They seem to *be fed up with everything & I expect especially at the nasty smacks delivered by us nearly every day. Deserters are fairly numerous.*

Sunday, 11th November 1917

Today we saw two Russian officers. They are fine looking fellows.

Were these officers emissaries from the Russian army encamped further up the Vilayet valley to prevent the Turks from retreating further north? There was a brief period of cooperation between the Russians and the British after the Czar's abdication in March, but it came to an end in November when the Bolsheviks took over. Having seen the writing on the wall, the officers could also have been deserters.

Yesterday we were all very surprised to see a lady drive into camp accompanied by a few officers. The lady turned out to be an American journalist who is touring round, although I don't imagine this to be a country to go touring in, even for the newspapers.

The nights are beginning to get very cold now.

17

Death of a General

The American journalist who arrived at Walter's camp in Baqubah was Eleanor Franklin Egan, the colourful war correspondent of the illustrated weekly magazine, *Saturday Evening Post*. Orphaned when she was a child, a one-time actress and a professional writer with a rich husband, she was a force to be reckoned with.

Eleanor had waited a month in Bombay before getting permission to go to Baghdad. She had pulled all the considerable strings she had at her disposal, held tea parties and attended formal dinners, persuasively putting her case to high-ranking officials while their tightly-corseted mensahibs made sure their tiaras weren't slipping.

She was determined to meet the elusive General Maude but was laughingly told she'd never get within a thousand miles of him.

For the next few days, while Eleanor makes her plans, Walter works hard and keeps his diary up to date.

Monday, 12th November 1917

Have been setting out two co-ordinated gauges in zinc. A very tedious job, especially as it is reversed!

Tuesday, 13th November 1917

We have heard of many cases of cholera at Baghdad. Some of the litho and printing tents are isolated. There are cases also of smallpox. With this news we feel rather thankful to be here.

Wednesday, 14th November 1917

Posted money order for £5 to Joe Povey. Worked on five plates and an establishment list of points on the map.

Walter is no longer lonely, thanks to Rex and his little dog, and has, he says, little news for Emma. So he embroiders his next letter with a few flowery sentiments.

3rd Corps HQ
Meso
Nov 1917

'My Darling Mother,

'Yesterday I had a letter from dear Jim, written at Newmarket, & such a nice little snap of Dorrie & himself. He has just the same cheerie old smile & has no doubt greatly improved in health after being with his dear folks in England.' (Jim was a victim of mustard gas at Ypres. He was left with a dry, hacking cough and his tall figure was permanently stooped by its effect on his lungs.)

'Did he go to London after his stay in hospital? I know how happy you would be to see his dear face again. Jim tells me of Billie's success when sitting for his first exam & I hope he is quite as successful in the final & I know we feel jolly proud of him. I hear that Susie is now staying at home with you & also has had her boy with her at 27. I hope dearest that you are quite well & don't worry about your soldier boys too much will you. Joe has sent me some letters including one of Mr Hankinson to Joe, in which I read all the news of Clarence Road.

'I am quite fit & strong & still enjoy my walks down by the river with my chum Rex Smith. Yesterday evening we went swimming & thoroughly enjoyed our dip in the cold water. Fancy bathing in England in November! I have been rather busy all this week but have written to Percy & Joe P. also to Mr Hankinson. I have sent five pounds to Joe Povey by Money Order, which he will change & let you have the cash for me. I hope you have received my previous money orders!

'I have a bed in my tent, a wicker affair made by Arabs, & with 2 sheets, 2 overcoats

& 2 blankets I manage to sleep quite comfortably.

'News is very scarce so consequently my letter is but small.

'I am enclosing a letter for Percy for you to send when you are writing to him.

'Now mother dearest I will say goodbye until next mail. God bless you dear, & my best love always.

'Yr. loving son, Walter'

By now Eleanor Egan had arrived in Baghdad, met General Maude and asked him if she might go to the front. 'You are at the front,' she was told. Babylon then? Maybe with a couple of armoured cars? This time, permission was refused.

However, he invited her to accompany him to a performance of *Hamlet*, to be performed in Arabic by a Jewish school. A platform had been set up in a Baghdad square, covered in Persian carpets and gleaming brocade. A colourful crowd had assembled: Jews, Persians, Arabs, Kurds, Syrians, Chaldeans and representatives of a dozen Eastern races, splendidly turned out in silk robes, turbans and tarbooshes, the women mostly unveiled.

The general and Mrs Egan must have been a noticeable contrast to the other concert-goers, and to one another: Eleanor, chatty and 'rather fat' – as she had been described by that other redoubtable woman author in Arabia at the time, the aristocratic Gertrude Bell – and tall, reserved General Maude, with his long, droopy moustache hiding his mouth. They had been there for some time before they realised that *Hamlet* was to be the eleventh event in the programme. If this worried the general, whose bed-time was ten o'clock, he did not show it. Coffee was served to them on a small table with two cups, a bowl of sugar and a jug of milk. General Maude politely helped himself to coffee and milk. Mrs Egan had coffee only. The entertainment went on until four o'clock in the morning and performers and audience alike were increasingly enthusiastic, with the children charmingly forgetting their words.

General Maude entered into the spirit of the evening before suddenly turning pale. He seemed very tired on the way back to his residence. Next day, Mrs Egan was surprised when he wasn't at lunch. He was a stickler for punctuality and she and his staff were worried. Later came the news that he had contracted cholera in its most virulent form through the untreated milk. He died next day. Rumours that he had been poisoned were given credibility by previous assassination attempts made on him but, as Mrs Egan said, he might so easily not have had milk in his coffee that the idea of a conspiracy was officially discounted.

The irony of the situation – in *Hamlet* the king is poisoned – gives the tragic event a Shakespearean twist. The general had refused a vaccination. A religious man, he thought God would protect him.

Thursday, 15th November 1917

Today we heard that Gen. Maude has been taken ill with cholera.

Friday, 16th November 1917

Had an aeroplane scare today, the warning, three blasts on the whistle, was sounded & soon after the alarm, one long & one short blast, at which we all left work and doubled to the trenches which are only a few yards from us. However we heard nothing from above & soon were back at work.

Saturday, 17th November 1917

I have been very busy lately compiling a map of the Qizil Ribat district and have had a host of air photos, reports, surveys etc. from which to gather information. I played hockey with staff & officers. Quite a good game & will help keep us from getting rusty.

Sunday, 18th November 1917

We, Rex & I, went for a long walk and then to the church tent. The new general was there, Gen. Maxwell having gone to G.H.Q.

The padre gave a fine address on Jerusalem & was very eloquent, touching on the history *of that city from the Babylonian period to the present day.*

Tonight the sad news reached us of the death of Gen. Maude.

Monday, 19th November 1917

Gen. Maude is to be buried today. His loss will be widely felt & regretted by all those who served under him out here.

We have had many reports of enemy planes around. Some have passed over Baghdad & others to the North-East of Baqubah and were firing only a few miles away, keeping our planes busy around the vicinity.

> 'The day after the general's funeral in Baghdad, a Turkish aeroplane flew low over the British residency and dropped a message of sympathy before making swiftly and safely away. A touching tribute from a gallant foe.' *(Sir Stanley Maude and other memories by Ms Stuart Menzies.)*

Tuesday, 20th November 1917

Worked hard at map today finishing off about midday. Played hockey with staff officers & clerks this evening.

Saturday, 24th November 1917

Issued with 2 pairs woollen knicks & undershirt, also mackintosh & serge slacks, part of winter clothing, plus ration of baccy 2 oz. + 1 bag matches!

Sunday 25th, November 1917

Memorial Service for Gen. Maude this morning taken by the area Padre (Archdeacon Day). Tonight the Gurkas' band played outside Gen. Maude's residence which is almost next door to us.

General Maude had proved to be a capable commander, popular with his men. Born in Gibraltar into a military family, educated at Eton and Sandhurst, he was a methodical and successful soldier. He lived simply, shunning the perks enjoyed by other generals.

His long droopy moustache is a noticeable feature in his photograph. Neither a confident handlebar twirl, like General Kitchener's, nor a narrow line of bristle from under the nose to the top of the lip favoured by dictators like Hitler and Robert Mugabe, General Maude's falls in a long fringe over his mouth, as soft as the hair on a baby's head.

Did his wife remember its soft touch on her lips when he bade her his final goodbye? Did he discreetly part it at the edges to stop it from flopping into the cup of coffee he drank on the fateful evening he spent with Mrs Egan? Did it conceal bad teeth, or perhaps reveal an unexpected tenderness of character unexpected in one of WW1's foremost warriors?

Whatever strategies are worked out, the outcome of a war often turns upon chance. If General Maude had had an early night, instead of going off to downtown Baghdad with Mrs Egan, he might never have caught cholera and died when he was still so badly needed to see his campaign through. Would the war in the Middle East have ended more satisfactorily and the ensuing legacy of disasters been avoided? Gertrude Bell wrote that, had he lived, 'there would have been a desperate tussle when administrative problems became more important than military'. Her own detractors could have claimed that treaties might have been agreed with more common sense and boundaries drawn up with deeper understanding than by following T E Lawrence's over-optimism and Gertrude Bell's arbitrary straight lines through much of Arabia.

Eleanor Egan wrote *The War in the Cradle of the World* after her tour of India and the Middle East. It was a bestseller and is still in print. It is not clear whether Walter ever read it; her gossipy style may not have appealed to him.

She had escaped General Maude's fate when he was infected by cholera during their evening together but Eleanor also died prematurely, in 1925 aged 48, of pneumonia. She was already sufficiently eminent to have the future president Herbert Hoover as one of her pall-bearers.

While Walter was in Mesopotamia, T E Lawrence was in Syria trying to convince the Arabs that the British were bringers of freedom. In his introduction to *The Seven Pillars of Wisdom*, his autobiography describing the part he played in the Arab/Turkish conflict, and the guilt and disillusion he felt afterwards about its outcome, Lawrence writes graphically about his feelings:

> 'Some of the evil of my tale may have been inherent in our circumstances. For years we lived anyhow with one another in the naked desert, under the indifferent heaven. By day the hot sun fermented us; and we were dizzied by the beating wind. At night we were stained by dew, and shamed into pettiness by the innumerable silences of stars.
>
> 'I am most sorry that I have not told what the non-commissioned of us did. They were but wonderful, especially when it is taken into account that they had

not the motive, the imaginative vision of the end, which sustained officers.'

I remember *The Seven Pillars of Wisdom* from when I was a child. A hardback with a slightly torn paper cover, it was squashed into a bookcase next to *The Valleys of the Assassins* by explorer Freya Stark whose writing Walter preferred. I doubt whether he would have thought of himself and his fellow non-commissioned soldiers as not having 'the motive, the imaginative vision of the end, which sustained officers'.

He would have regarded Tennyson's views of their motive and vision of the end as closer to the truth.

Not though the soldier knew
Someone had blundered.
Theirs not to make reply,
Theirs not to reason why,
Theirs but to do and die.

18

The Draughtsman's Desk

Walter's most interesting maps may survive in some dusty official archive in London. But only one early example, probably done in India as a test, turned up in the linen bag. Even this shows a steady hand and the competent lettering that helped him to become a recognised commercial artist and achieve a successful career.

Standing in the corner of my workroom is the draughtsman's desk at which he created many of his later drawings and sketches. It accompanied him from the commercial art studio where he worked during the 1930s to a London advertising agency and from there, on his retirement, to his home.

The desk is made of unvarnished oak. Unadorned and functionally elegant, its main feature is a large, rectangular wooden board, supported by an adjustable frame to allow it to go flat like a table, to tilt like a desk or to be set upright like an easel. There is a drawer at one side – pull it out and the top slides back to make a shelf where Walter lined up his pen-holders, sets of nibs and a bottle of black Indian ink.

Some of his treasured tools are still there: a slide rule, spirit level, T-square, compasses and a rusting double-edged knife. Some intricately-curved shapes cut from thin sheet of boxwood were used to trace rounded corners or to draw perfect circles. He'd bought most of them second-hand but some may have been a legacy from his war days in Mesopotamia, where tools like these had been around for hundreds of years.

Through their use, helped by his ability to draw and a good head for geometry, Walter soon became good at calculating distances. His task was made easier by another time-honoured tool of the trade: the theodolite – a small telescope on legs with horizontal and vertical scales to pinpoint the precise location of a particular landmark. Walter and his fellow map-makers would set one up during forays up the River Tigris to help assess changes wrought by the devastation to canals, irrigation systems and bridges during the floods and fighting of the previous year. Where they could, they would climb to the top of a ruined tower or broken bridge to plot their angles via a group of abandoned orange groves or a deserted army encampment shimmering on a distant bend in the river.

But the biggest help of all were two developments that were revolutionising cartography in the early 20th century: the camera and the aeroplane.

For their time the early images produced by aerial photography were amazingly accurate. Footsteps in the sand were visible when images taken at 1,500 feet were enlarged.

Cameras powerful enough to take aerial photographs were enormously bulky and had to be fixed to the side of the fuselage of a rickety two-seater bi-plane. The pilot flew as near as he could to the target while the cameraman behind him would lean perilously out of his seat, take aim, and click.

Sometimes there were errors in interpretation, when, for instance, a German aerial photographer thought he had captured a scene of panic among British soldiers on the ground when, in fact, they were playing football. But large areas could for the first time be seen and recorded from the air. This was a huge advantage in a flat, often featureless country like Mesopotamia where you could often see no further than the ranks of reeds along the bank of the river.

The stern Major C P Gunter, whose reputation had made Walter nervous when he was in Baghdad, was an innovative cartographer who devised a system of aiming artillery fire at specific points in the trenches behind Turkish battle lines. Four photographers on the British side took pictures of shell bursts over the lines simultaneously with a cameraman in the air. These images were co-ordinated with an aerial map of the Turks' complex maze of trenches. Points observed in this way were then registered on the map by pins and used to match up the strips of photography like a highly-sophisticated jigsaw puzzle.

This was where Walter came in. Once he had the strips in place the map took shape and he made a careful tracing before producing a meticulous pen-and-ink copy, which he would then reduce in size, re-draw and etch onto a metal plate, reversing it so it would come out the right way round.

He really preferred to be working out in the field but it was pleasantly warm in the litho tent and once he got to work he became so fired with enthusiasm that he'd carry on far into the night to complete a project.

Map-making was not his only occupation when Christmas began to draw near:

Friday, 29th November 1917

Finished a calendar for 3rd Corps, which I drew on zinc plate. It seems to please everyone so that's good.

More ominously, he continues: *Fired a course of revolver shooting this afternoon with fair results considering first time.*

It was unusual these days for Walter to be involved in anything as directly military as shooting practice but it could be explained by the activities of Bolshevik whistle-blowers in the Russian press. A secret agreement had been drawn up in 1916 between the French and UK governments, with the assent of Russia, in order to define their areas of control in the Middle East once the Ottoman Empire was defeated. The terms of the Sykes-Picot Agreement, as it is known, were a secret no longer now that the Bolsheviks had taken over Czarist Russia.

Whilst the Agreement was being negotiated, the British High Commissioner in Egypt had unwittingly promised Emir Sharif Hussein ibn Ali, the last king of the Hashemites to rule Mecca and the most influential of all the Arab leaders, that the entente would support the creation of a confederation of Arab States in greater Syria. In return, King Hussein agreed that Arab forces would join them in rising up against the hated Ottoman Turks. Accordingly he led the ultimately successful Arab revolt of 1916 – the revolt in which Lawrence of Arabia played a prominent part.

The Bolsheviks had allowed the contents of the Sykes-Picot Agreement to be made public and the terms were published in *Izvestia* and *Pravda*. The British were highly embarrassed by the revelations, the Arabs were deeply shocked by what looked to them like a British betrayal, and the Turks were eventually forced into a peace they would overturn. On the part of the French, François Georges-Picot, the Picot of the Agreement, felt he owed no responsibility to King Hussein as he had not taken part in the Hussein/McMahon transaction.

This political unease had led to increased army activity by the British to protect the northern border of the part of Mesopotamia destined for British control. The Turks were still there and fighting back.

Sunday, 2nd December 1917

Advance party from 3rd Corps & all staff officers have gone off to Qal'at Shergat (north of Baqubar, about 50 miles south of Mosul) today.

Tuesday, 4th December 1917

Walked to Baqubah & visited most parts of the village. Returning passed some of our Red X wagons bearing wounded to Baghdad. Fighting is taking place towards the Persian border around Altin Kopru. Our casualties are 10 killed & some wounded. We took 160 prisoners – 2 field guns & 2 machine guns.

The towns Walter mentions had long been the locations of unresolved conflict, lying as they do on strategic trade routes of northern Mesopotamia and peopled by tribes whose culture and religion were different from those of their neighbours. It was left to Gertrude Bell, who had arrived in Baghdad from Cairo in April 1917, to try to sort out the ensuing mess.

A strange choice, perhaps, as the mediator between the various factions. First of all she was a woman, then she was a member neither of the British government nor the army. Sir Mark Sykes, co-author of the Sykes-Picot Agreement, made sexist remarks about her, saying she was 'flat-chested and a blathering ass.'

She was certainly not the latter. Gertrude had a long line of academic qualifications, including a first from Oxford in modern history. She spoke Arabic more fluently than T E Lawrence and had, after twenty years in the Middle East, more affinity with many of the Arabs of the desert than with her compatriots. Her billowing muslin costumes and wide English hats above an unruly shock of blonde curls were no bar to the respect in which the Arabs held her.

She had misgivings, wondering in a letter to her father whether the entente's proposals might do more harm than good. Nevertheless, she felt the Arabs were not ready to rule themselves and when, a few years later, she sat down with selected leaders and a set of maps, the boundaries she proposed made little more allowance for ethnic and religious differences than those of the Sykes-Picot Agreement. The troubled regimes of Iraq, Syria and the Lebanon were to be the result of what was an impossible task.

There was no doubt that the old Ottoman Empire was finished as a world power. The position of the Germans and Austro-Hungarians was less certain. The arrival of the Americans had given the Allies a boost to morale and their financial and industrial aid was taking hold. Nevertheless the Germans and their allies were not going to give up without a struggle.

Meanwhile, bombing raids over London had intensified. They drew nearer to Archibald Road as the winter nights closed in.

27 Archibald Rd.
Tufnell Park
London N.7
Dec. 6th 1917, 6.00am

'My dearest Wallie,

'All this week I have been trying to get a quiet hour to write to you dear but there have been so many visitors that the time has not been my own till I have felt too tired, then have gone off to bed, not that I mind the visitors coming, you know I like it, but this morning just before five we were woken by Police whistles & Gun Fire so you can tell dear by this that we, i.e. Vera, Sue & I, were not long dressing & getting down into the Kitchen. These sorts of visitors we don't like, they are too noisy, just at present they have cleared off, but of course you never know if a fresh batch is coming.

'This morning the moonlight is beautiful but it is very cold, quite a frost, and we have made a good fire & have had some tea, so we are feeling better able to receive the next batch if they can get through. Our air service is splendid & old Fritz has something to do, to catch them napping, but oh my dear how we do long for all these horrors to cease & to have our loved ones home again, & to the Boys that are away it must seem an endless time. Still we have our letters dear & they must cheer the hearts of thousands, only fancy what a dreadful blank it would seem without them. I am afraid, yes I know, I have not written so often, dear there are excuses but I won't bother you with them, only I thank all my dear Boys who have written me so often & lovingly.

'Last Friday we had a surprise visitor, Clarence Oxenham, the youngest Son (23) of my dear old Friend in NZ. He came straight away from the trenches, for 14 days leave, after being 19 months on & off in the Firing Line. He has gone now to Scotland for a few days but is making this his home & we are very pleased to have him, he is a nice bright well-spoken fellow & the girls get a fine time. He takes them out & buys things to bring home & the other night he took us all (Billy included) to the Palace Cinema, Balcony Seats front row, about 2/- now & a nice Box of

Chocks included. Well dear you know I am making him feel at home.

'Yesterday I had another surprise, I was going to Boscastle Rd. to Tea & first had to get to the end of Huddleston Rd. when another soldier Boy came suddenly round the corner, in the form of Bert Handley, so we trotted home again, (I am now glad of the help of anyone's arm). He looked fine & had a comparatively safe job, in the Offices of the Flying Corps France. He just came up from Harrow on his own, to visit us all. He has been home some few days now, but they are all coming up before he goes away again.

'I am rather expecting that Percy & Jamie may be home at Xmas time, then, if Billy is still here, it will be fine. He is still waiting for his ship to come back, it has been taken over by Government & is at present with the Fleet in the North Sea. All his belongings including his Violin are on it, so if he has to go to another ship, I shall have to fit him out again. I think I told you dear that the Company gave him the privilege of studying for his Mates Certificate, he says he passed the examinations but the Board of Trade said he was too young & must pass again after he is nineteen – during this time his ship went off without him, & he has been waiting ever since; just a fine Holiday for him but any day now he may have to go off.'

Emma breaks off her letter at this point. She has made light of the early morning raid but that evening she has some bad news:

'6.30pm

'We have had a quiet day dear, & hope to go bed early & get a good night's rest, but there is something a little sad to tell you.

'Poor old Carrie died suddenly during the Raid. She was quite well the day before & was at Auntie Minnie's to Tea, & went for a little walk to see the shops & went to bed quite all right. When the guns started, she came down from her Top Room to the landlady's & had only just time to get in, & sit in a chair, when she died.

'Auntie came round to us about 12, & naturally was very much upset. She said, it was a strange thing, but they were talking about Raids, & Carrie said, I believe if we have another like the last it would kill me. She had a very weak heart, the Doctor said, so there will be no inquest.

'Poor dear faithful kind soul. We shall all miss her very much.

'About a fortnight ago dear I received a letter from you. It is dated Sept 23rd. You had just received your first batch of letters & were so pleased at receiving same, in it you spoke dear of sending some money but I have had no notice of it from the P.O. yet. The letter contained a small photo of Tregonning which I will take care of dear. I am glad to hear he is well & I trust has not had to go back to France. I see dear I have a later letter & the last from you up to this day. It is dated Oct. 3rd and in it you tell me you have sent two separate money orders, one for £2 and another for £2.10s.0d.

'I have not received either, is there any mistake dear? What a strange thing dear, the ink is not dry yet on what I have written and the Postman has just brought the Money Orders, so I will Bank the £2.10s.0d. for you dear. The other two pounds I will split into four, 10/- for Vie, a present each to Harold & Minnie, something useful up to 10/- each & the rest for myself. I will let you know next time what I buy. It is ever so good of you dear to do this & I know you will be pleased to split the present you intended for Harold into two. I wonder if you know that young Minnie was married about a month ago to Sidney Hogg. They are living at Tulse Hill. I shall be going to see them shortly and will let them choose a present from you. Percy gave them a small Dinner Set and I a Fire Screen. They had a large number of presents – I must hurry up as the post limit is near, am enclosing a note I had from Jamie this morning & Percy is going on all right. All the girls are well & send love.

'Vera is living with us & going to Biz in the Brecknorth Rd. at a Builders as a Shorthand Typist. She is very happy with us, but could not get on well with her Mother, so the change will do them both good.

'Now dear I will wish you a Happy Xmas & may the New Year bring us peace.

'With my fondest love & many kisses & may God Guide & Guard you dear Son. Be careful the Heat does not upset you dear but take great care of yourself, to come home to us all strong.

'Ever your loving Mother,

E.B.'

The end for poor Carrie almost coincided with the final bombing raids on London. The

Germans had lost three Gotha bombers during the raid of December 6th, one of them on the way home. Defences were improving with brighter, more accurate searchlights and better trained night-fighter pilots. This is a newspaper report after a raid on 18th December:

> *Twenty-seven defending machines of the best performance went up, and three combats took place. As a result, one of the Gothas was so damaged that it fell into the sea off Folkestone and was destroyed. On this night the new "Giant" aeroplane came over London for the first time. It dropped a bomb in Lyall Street, near Eaton Square, making a large crater but doing little serious damage.*

Perhaps, at last, the horrors of war were on the point of ceasing and the boys would soon be home.

Tuesday, 11th December 1917

To-day the weather is glorious. A fresh wind is sighing through the palms just beyond the camp, & chasing little white puffs of cloud across the blue sky. The air is delightfully clear & crisp & the sun just adds that warmth that makes one feel as if he has partaken of some refreshing wine. Had to break ice to get a walk this morning.

Wednesday, 12th December 1917

Cold spell continues. Ice much thicker.

Thursday, 13th December 1917

Colder than ever. I lifted a complete shape in ice from our bucket. This weather is helping greatly to stamp out the cholera that has infected Baghdad.

Wednesday, 19th December 1917

Rained very heavily last night & this morning. The ground is in an awful condition. Very slippery & the heavy mud cakes one's boots.

Many tents have been flooded owing chiefly to indifferent drainage. The earth holds the water on the surface for a very long time – in fact I find that the moisture has soaked 9 inches into the ground.

Sunday, 23rd December 1917

Very miserable outlook this morning, damp, heavy mist & cold.

Monday, 24th December 1917

Played chess with Rex this evening. But both of us retired after a long drawn-out game. The Cheshams sang carols outside the Officers' mess & we could just hear them & it sounded quite nice.

Tuesday, 25th December 1917

This morning is lovely & just like English Xmas weather. Went for a delightful walk down by the river. Five-course dinner ending with a portion of excellent Christmas pudding, sent by friends in India to the troops out here. In the evening Cull, who is my tent fellow, & I made our tent cosy & then invited two chums to join us in a game of bridge.

Friday, 28th December 1917

Mail came this afternoon. A lovely letter from Mabs & one from Mr Hankinson & another from Mrs Agland.

Sunday, 30th December 1917

Walked into Qalat trying to find track leading across neck of land stretching between big bend of River Dyalah. We struck the wrong route & wandered through the village, which is terribly dirty. On outskirts there are heaps of dead donkeys, muck heaps etc.

On this rather despondent note, the second and last of Walter's war diaries comes to an end.

19

Keep the Home Fires Burning

'There's a silver lining
Through the dark clouds shining,
Turn the dark cloud inside out
Till the boys come home.'
(Lyrics by Lena Guilbert Ford,
music by Ivor Novello)

'Percy again wounded & in England, poor old chappie, but still it is nice to know he is progressing favourably, away from the trenches for a time. Jimmy, is he still in Newmarket? I wonder if they were able to be with you on Christmas Day? I thought of you then, Mother dear, & pictured you seated by the fire in the evening, just as we used to when we were all together.'

So wrote Walter on New Year's Day 1918, after his fourth Christmas away from his family. Concerned about the health of his two sick brothers, Percy with cancer, though nobody ever said so, and Jimmy suffering from the effects of mustard gas – Walter is aching with nostalgia for home and missing his family more than ever.

As his correspondence with Emma draws to a close he writes a long overdue letter to Mr Hankinson: 'just these few lines,' he promises, but his enthusiasm runs away with him and the last of his war letters turns into the following narrative. Surprisingly, he finds himself in India once more.

For the first time since he left home he is on leave but neither the reasons nor the 'unfortunate circumstances' he mentions are clear.

The letter has been censored. Someone has scrawled: 'From a 2nd Cpl. In Litho Section, Mesopotamia, from a letter sent to England' across the top. Walter heads the letter 'August. 18, Kirkee India'. Someone else has written in the margin – 'Return to Mr Hankinson, 60 Haverstock Hill, Hampstead NW3.' Whole sections are crossed through but do not hide the words underneath.

'Dear Mr Hankinson,

'Just these few lines to send you & friends at Clarence Rd, my best wishes. I hope that you have good news from all the boys & that Norman Taylor is quite well again.

'Since I left Mesopotamia last April I have not received any home mails except those that arrived there during the first two weeks of my absence. The remainder being kept for me, so if you have sent any letters likely to reach there during the months that have passed, you will understand why I have not acknowledged them.

'When I left Meso I had no idea that I should remain in India for so long a time, indeed I fully expected to return there at the end of June, but certain unfortunate circumstances have delayed my return although I have never known when an order would come through to send us back and even now one cannot tell when such an order may come and consequently I have to hold myself in readiness.

'I do feel so very lonely without my letters from dear Mother & the home folks. These letters form the chief happiness of my life now that I am away from them all, & now I feel like one in exile. However when I was with Joe he gave me all his letters to read & it was from him I learnt of Jim & Dorrie's marriage at our church on that notable day. Joe has a copy of the service. I have one awaiting me yonder.

'I also heard of Percy's marriage. The news came as a very happy surprise.

'There will be changes in the old home when we return, but one could only wish them to be so, & pray that those days will come soon when, please God, we shall return to our friends again.

'I hope you are in good health & that you have good attendances at the Church Services. I hear that you have a number of new friends in the congregation, which must be very heartening to you in these days when so many of us are far away.'

Having unburdened himself of thoughts of home, Walter relives another remarkable rail journey in the country he has come to love.

'I arrived in India on April 28th, & after a glorious journey by train over the magnificent ghats I arrived at Kirkee where I spent two days arranging various matters before proceeding to Mussourie. I came on leave with my friend (Rex Smith) & we had arranged to spend our time at this station, unless I heard from Joe anything that would necessitate altering my arrangements.

'However in the early morning of June 1st I was seated in the Breakfast Car of the Bombay Mail passing down the ghats, now bathed in sunlight that gleamed on the huge red walls of rock & sparkled in the running waters of tiny falls that leapt down deep chasms until they were lost in the dense foliage of trees at the foot of these huge hills. I left this train at Kalyan Junction & there boarded the Punjab Mail en route for Dehra Dun, the terminal for the hills some 1,500 miles North of Kirkee. I had travelled over this same route before with the 25th Londons, but although I now travelled in the luxury of 2nd class I did not enjoy the journey so well as when with Joe & about six other fellows we crowded into a smelly old 3rd class native carriage. But then we travelled in December, when all nature is at its best, refreshed and full of beautiful plants after the life-giving monsoons, whereas now every living thing awaited the rains.

'The forest trees were shrivelled & bare of leaf & the cultivated plains, bereft of the lovely green & gold of rice & corn fields, now lay barren & scorched under a tortured sun, whilst the great broad rivers over which we sped were shrunken into mere streams, leaving great white beds of staring sand on either side.

'After travelling two and a half days I arrived at Derha Dun & from here we travelled by motor to Raj Pur, along a pretty road, well shaded by spreading banyan trees & slender bamboo with here & here a pretty bungalow, half hidden behind masses of flowering creepers, whilst straight in front of us rose the foothills of the Himalayas, soaring straight up from the wooded slopes of the plains & dwarfing everything below by their hugeness and strength.

'Presently we came to Raj Pur, a pretty little town at the foot of the hills.

'From here to Mussoorie, 6,500 feet above, lines of coolies labour daily up the one rocky road, eight miles in length, bearing all kinds of bulky cases. Indeed these men carry everything from the plains to Mussoorie & one is astonished at the enormous loads they will carry, even pianos. These bulky weights are transported by these means, no vehicles being allowed to ascend the road.

'I made my journey from Raj Pur on the back of a stocky mountain pony, luckily a quiet animal, so I had no fears of being suddenly pitched over the roadside.

'There were many other people climbing up the mountain-side. The road was ablaze with many coloured sunshades beneath which ladies reclined in quaint-looking doolies (a sort of sedan chair), carried by four coolies. Also many menfolk who like myself were astride ponies.

'We & the doolies formed a caravan on the road. The ponies, no matter how their riders may urge them on, will only proceed at walking pace & delight in following one behind the other on the edge of the road nearest the downslope.

'After zig-zagging up the first three miles of road, the air becomes appreciably cooler & one enters for the first time the beautiful oak woods which rise & fall with the slopes of the hills on all sides. Lovely wild roses & many flowering shrubs grow by the roadside & even when the road emerges from the woods and trails over some rocky shoulder of the mountain, one sees rocks above whilst a clear view of the plains below is obtained. They lie stretched out in glorious panorama with here & there white towns and cities peeping out from dark masses of trees, whilst the far-reaching arms of the Ganges & Jimna Rivers leave the hills & stretch out across the plains. Away in the distance one sees the outline of the Siwalik Hills & beyond them in a deep blue smudge on the horizon lie the greater plains of India.

'Presently we climbed over a great rocky shoulder of the mountain & on reaching the other side we came to a few cottages where everyone stopped for refreshment & to rest & water the ponies.

'We had now reached the heart of the hills which arose everywhere around us, clad with mighty forests of stately oaks & the great heights clad with darker green deodars. From this place onward the road passed through most glorious scenery. Everywhere arose the tall moss-grown oak trees. Huge rocks overgrown with lichen and ivy were strewn over the hillsides.

'Here & there we passed tastefully built bungalows surrounded by lovely gardens filled with sweet peas & roses & other sweet-scented flowers, & at last we sighted Mussoorie, its white bungalows gleaming amid the trees, & after a hard climb we entered this charming city in the hills. One by one the little caravans fell away, each one going to his or her destination.'

The next sentence has been crudely crossed out by the censor's pencil but Walter's writing, in pen, is still easily legible. 'I found The Soldiers' Furlough Home perched high up on a wide grassy ledge, commanding an excellent view over the plains, & arrived at the pretty bungalow. I soon found my friends & after being introduced to Mr and Mrs Stevens, who manage this happy home, I settled down & was soon made to feel comfy after having demolished a huge dinner.

'I spent three weeks at Mussoorie & thoroughly enjoyed every day of my stay there. My friends and I had many delightful picnics, descending little zigzag paths that trailed beneath beautiful woods of oak, ash & wayfaring trees, to where a splashing waterfall emptied itself into a deep pool of crystal water before it leapt merrily over the rocks and down the mountainside.

'Here we would seek out a spot to spread out the contents of a luncheon basket & then, leaving a coolie to make ready & get tea, we would go exploring in the great silent woods, chancing upon many perfect, fairy-tale places & gathering huge bunches of wild berries & flowers & picking a few wild strawberries & raspberries, the latter being very delicious. Then we would seek a deep pool below some cascade & spend a jolly hour splashing about in the pure, invigorating water. From the rocks round about, we added to our bunches of flowers, formed of many varieties including the delicate maidenhair fern. At last we would return to our rendezvous, more than ready for our lunch.

'Sometimes we set out early in the morning, with haversacks loaded with eatables, and climbed high up the steep rocky ascent of some near peak. At the top we would survey the wonderful panorama of the plains at 8,000 and 9,000 feet below whilst in the opposite direction one could see the massive outlines of the Himalayas.

'Unfortunately we never had a clear view of the snows, except on one memorable evening, although even to see the majestic outlines of this mighty range, lifted high into the heavens, is an experience I shall never forget. But oh, to see the same mountains when the air is clear & the white mists have lifted. To see the eternal snows kindled by the fiery glow of the setting sun, the rosy light on their glowing peaks flushing the heavens about them, whilst deep down the mountain side one sees the utter dark of night slowly creeping up from the unknown, until it shrouds those glowing peaks in dark velvet and the moon comes with shafts of golden light. Those mighty seats of the gods are lost to view & we must labour down to the little town below, gladdened & awed by the majesty of the mountains.

'Another day my two friends and I set out on horseback along a wooded road, strewn with loveliness, until, after riding for an hour or so, we came out of the woods &

entered into very wild and bare mountain lands. Two great ranges of mountain divided by a deep valley now faced us & we could see the road trailing ahead for miles. We now rode along a road cut into the mountain, on one side was a sheer drop of many thousand feet & on the other a solid rock wall.

'The road was quite narrow & the sensation experienced when riding along it with nowhere to look except at the giddy depths below or the forbidding mountain sides above proved most exciting. We fully enjoyed this part of the ride, travelling two and a half hours without seeing a hut, or a tree, or any sign of humans, but at last we saw a hillman's hut near the roadside and here we left our horses and proceeded on foot, intending to climb a high peak to get a view over the land.

'We had walked about half a mile when we were much startled at seeing a rock come crashing down the mountainside above us. We had lost sight of it for a few seconds when suddenly it appeared leaping far out over a ledge just above us, & descending with terrific force, crashing down onto the road about 20 yards from where we stood, and then leaping far out beyond the road & down the steep descent below, where we could hear it crashing and rebounding among other rocks.

'I am afraid that this little incident rather dampened our resolve to climb further, & after continuing our way for a short time we sat down beneath an immense slab of rock and watched the cloud shadows racing over the mountain sides & then, after eating a few sandwiches, we climbed down to the road & returned to the hillman's hut. Our horses were ready for us & we lost no time in starting back for Mussoorie as heavy clouds were rolling up from the valley in dense black masses & an occasional heavy peal of thunder came echoing up among the hills.

'We were still on the narrow mountain road when the storm which had threatened burst upon us.

'At first I thought that the deafening noise of falling rain & bursts of thunder would frighten the horses but they carried on at a slow job-trot & did not seem to take any notice of the raging elements.

'When we finally reached Mussoorie, we were drenched to the skin, but a quick change into dry clothes & a hot dinner soon put everything right & we devoted the rest of the evening to a game of chess.

'My friends & I had many rides & picnics together during the three weeks that I remained at Mussoorie & one early morning at the end of those glorious days I said goodbye to all my friends & set out down 8 miles of mountain road to the plains.'

The scenery has Walter under its spell, just as it had when he caught his first glimpse of the distant mountains across the plain of Burhan. But here there are no long marches with heavy army equipment to carry, no parades at dawn. He's free to ramble through the hills or explore the countryside by horseback and, joy of joys, experience the pleasure of a full stomach after years of army rations and constantly feeling hungry. Hot dinners, lunches, picnics stopping here and there for tea – Walter's cup is full to the brim. And if that were not enough, another delightful event is to make a perfect ending to his stay in India.

'Arrived at Derha Dun I boarded a train for Jutogh. I had previously arranged to meet

Joe there & spend the remaining week of my leave with him at the barracks as he was unable to get away to Mussoorie.

'Jutogh is situated about 5 miles in the hills, just below Simla, & to reach it one can either journey up 52 miles of road or by a tiny railway called the Kalka-Simla railway.

'It is a wonderful little railway & climbs tremendous gradients & negotiates very acute bends & angles besides thundering through 100 tunnels on its way from Kalka to Simla. The scenery from beginning to end is truly glorious. One passes over deep ravines where babbling streams splash down to the valleys beneath which cultivated fields are cunningly laid out in terraces, one above the other. One has an impression of a vast garden laid out in green & gold carpets, with here & here little white houses nestling beneath the trees, & all around & far away in the distance rise immense hills, always changing in aspect as the train winds round one of the numerous curves.

'I met dear Joe while he was walking from the company orderly room to the Band Bungalow which is built high up on a hill.'

From now on the word 'Joe' has been crossed out by the censor and replaced by 'J...'

'He was surprised to see me so early (I left Kalka at 1.30am & he had intended to come down to the station to meet me in the afternoon). Of course we were delighted to meet each other again & many were the questions that each asked the other as to what had occurred during the long lapse of time since we parted; of my folks & news, & that night I slept next to J..., just as I used to when I first came to India.

'We had many long walks & talks during that happy week & many a pleasant evening in Simla, usually finishing up at the theatre in Simla where J... was playing, & then a four mile walk back to Jutogh in the moonlight beneath the spreading branches of the Himalayan oaks.'

The whole of the next sentence has a wavy line scrawled over it in pen.

'No doubt J... has described Simla to you in his previous letters. It is a lovely town indeed, built as..........'

The page ends here and Walter's impression of Simla as it was in 1918 has been lost. Walter was in full descriptive flow so it's doubtful whether the letter ends with a description of Simla. Is his leave extended further or was he by now on his way back to Bombay and Mesopotamia?

A letter from Emma written in December 1918 assumes the latter, having as she says heard from him in October that he was on his way back to GHQ.

'Oh the joy of it,' she writes, her hand a little shaky. 'At last we can think that next year our boys may come home after the seeming never-ending wait.

'Did you have much excitement over the Armistice? I was just going out when the Sirens and Guns went off. At first I thought it was another Raid & it took me some time to get over the shivers but when at last I did get out there was great excitement in the Streets and the Flags were being put out like magic and little 2 penny ones were actually being sold for 8 pence.'

That day, 11th November, is to pass into vernacular memory as Poppy Day.

'I did not expect anyone to call but such a lot of people came in with all sorts of music and noise. Harold was the leader and they kept me very merry & the next night they came again and we finally finished up with cards.'

'This is Sunday December 8th, dear. Such a damp, misty miserable day out of doors but here in my bedroom I have a nice fire and I am trying to pick up with my writing, which is quite gone wrong. I forget even if I have told you anything about Susie's wedding.

'The fact is about a fortnight before the Wedding Sue and I got the flu and neither of us would give up. Sue got worse so that when she got to Eastbourne for her Honeymoon she nearly collapsed & Jack had to fetch the Dr. He ordered her to be poulticed Night & Day & told her afterwards it was only because she had a good constitution that she pulled through. She was in Bed for nearly a fortnight. Ruby went & nursed her the first week & Jack made a good nurse. At the end of nearly four weeks he brought her home, nearly well again.

'I really would have been glad for the Wedding to be put off but Sue would not hear of it. Everything went off A1, & we had a big Party. Gertie & Vin came, so I should have had all the girls but Daisy and her girlies went down & had to be in bed. (They are quite well now.) Then there were the Conerys. Marjorie, Laura & Mrs. C were very bad and Sylvia had to nurse them. But I am glad to tell you that Charley came. He happened to be in Hospital at Barnet so got some leave. He was looking very well considering he had given a quart of his blood for another man's sake, & that was the reason for him being in Hospital to pull up his strength. I believe he is still there. There were several others. Poor Winnie was very queer, although she was Bridesmaid, she was only just over a bad attack. Jim was expected to be with us, but just at the last minute all leave was cancelled for the North of London owing to the flu, & Louey & Emma at Woolwich dared not risk coming. Still dear as I say, we had a large Party & everything was A1 but for the Bride, who could not be so bright. I only wonder how she went through it.

'For myself dear I was better that week but worse the next & so on up & down till now. The Dr. says I must stop in my room till all traces of the cold have left me so I am just going to nurse myself up and see if I can get through for Xmas.'

Although Emma claims they were down with flu, one of Daisy's 'girlies' was at the wedding: the indefatigable Doris, who writes later that:

'Auntie Sue was married in a fox fur muff and a little brocade hat. She had flu so the night before her wedding she was very ill. In the afternoon I went with Uncle Jack, her husband, to the Palladium – my first visit to a Music Hall Matinee. Grandma said, "Take Doris, Sue is too ill in bed." We saw the famous comedian George Robey and I had on a grey coat, black beaver-trimmed hat (it lasted 20 years) and my first black handbag, black woollen gym stockings, I forget what frock – probably the brown striped velvet my Dad bought from Dickens and Jones – he did occasionally buy us very good clothes and our mother, Daisy, made us some very nice ones. I remember blue velvets – midnight blue. Sylvia had forget-me-nots she embroidered on hers around the neck and cuffs and I had scarlet pimpernels. We always wore them on Winter Sundays and white and blue striped in summers (hat time). Our clothes lasted till we outgrew them or a special occasion came along. Fussy ones with green shamrocks embroidered on them – pretty silk ones.'

Was it the flu that made Emma forget about Doris? She must have been very unwell to have been forsaken by her normally excellent memory.

Modern research suggests the pandemic was a virulent variety of bird or swine flu which spread quickly throughout Europe from rotting corpses and vermin in the trenches. It reached London in the summer of 1918, infecting the crowds celebrating the end of the Great War. It broke out in the United States and Asia. World-wide fatalities were estimated at 20-50 million, with 500 million infected, compared with 38 million killed in the War. It was known as 'Spanish flu' because the numbers of victims were made public in Spain but repressed in Britain, France, Germany and the United States. Treatment was very basic – Sue's poultice was probably warmed-up kaolin applied to a cloth and wrapped around her chest to ease her congestion.

Emma does not allow the effects of her own bout of illness to get her down. She continues:

'I am enclosing Percy's last letter dear, so that will give you a little more news than I feel I can write & dear will you pass it on to dear Joe. I am writing him just a few lines.

'Once again I must thank you for writing so regularly. You see dear it helps me from worrying. Joe too is very good & so between you I know just how you are.

'I have just received your October letter & rejoice with you dear for I know how glad you must feel that you are on your way back to Head Quarters & work again, till the happy day arrives that you set sail for home

& indeed I shall be one of the happiest of Mothers, to get you all home once more.

'How about that little dog Jim? Will they allow you to bring him? Did you really take him with you for your holiday trip? I guess he has been a comfort. Well I shall just love to have him but I'm afraid dear they won't let him come.

'I expect to have a quiet Xmas, but you know dear it will be happy with the thoughts that my dear ones are spared to me & that soon I may welcome them Home. Jim is still at Tunbridge Wells but hopes to get his discharge soon. Trusting you will have a Happy Xmas & keep well in health. God bless you dear Son,

'Love from all & a big kiss from

'Your own loving Mother E.B.'

Emma's offer to take his little dog Jim would have saddened Walter. Jim was dead. She was right – he wasn't allowed to go to England. Walter was ordered to have him shot.

He asked a friend with a good aim and a steady hand to kill him. The first shot only wounded him in the shoulder.

Walter would never forget the expression of sorrow in his eyes as he turned to him before the last fatal bullet.

Nothing is known of Walter's return journey to England in 1919 – only the brief memory of what he told my brother and me. As they approached the white cliffs of Dover, he threw his rusty rifle and battered pith helmet into the sea.

20

Walter finds his feet

Walter can never resist the urge to write. From a surviving notebook, together with a flimsy receipt and the fragment of a letter he has squirrelled away in the linen bag, we know enough to imagine his homecoming: Emma, who hardly ever cries, mingling tears with kisses and laughter, James smiling damply as he grasps Walter's hands in his own, and Sister Vi producing an awkward hug and a huge fruit cake. The celebrations go on for weeks, neighbours drop in and people Walter has never even met come up in the street to shake him by the hand. 'Well done, young man!'

The war has been won. Now the celebrations are over, Walter has peace to contend with.

He's come back to a much smaller family unit than the one he left behind at the beginning of the war. As he'd anticipated, there have been many changes to the old home now that all his brothers and sisters, except for Vi and Billie, are married. Vi is still living at home. Percy and Betty, who married in early 1919, bought the house at 27 Archibald Road and divided it into two flats, taking over the ground floor for themselves, with Emma, James, Violet and now Walter living upstairs. Although Emma struggles to climb the high flight of stairs to the first floor, she considers it a sacrifice worth making for Percy who is always so short of breath.

Walter finds the arrangement strange at first, but he likes his new room at the top of the house. It has a large window with a view over a jumble of narrow green gardens and red-roofed houses. Natural daylight means he no longer has to squint over his drawings the way he used to in the dark semi-basement room he shared with Joe.

Violet has a day-job as a housekeeper and cooks and cleans for Emma and James when she gets home. There are no more Monday visits from the washer-woman who before the war worked all day in the scullery.

Walter worries about keeping the household together with Percy so ill, his mother's strength failing and very little money coming in. He must find work, but competition is fierce. 'Hardly a thing doing,' he confides in his notebook:

'When I am not at home drawing I am running in and out all over town with my portfolio, dodging into studios and printers, etc.'

'One meets all kinds of people. The other day near St. Clement Danes I was passing a pavement artist who greeted me with a "Cheerio mate" and he was so smiling and friendly I might have considered sharing his place on the pavement, although even he might not have welcomed a competitor for the humble copper!'

There are many other ex-soldiers looking for jobs. Some of them tramping the streets have the haggard, shell-shocked faces of those who have suffered in the trenches. Some of them have sunk to their knees with no energy left to beg. Can this be Prime Minister Lloyd George's 'land fit for heroes'?

It is hard to come to terms with life in 'civvy street' after so long in uniform but at least Walter has a roof over his head and a family to give him moral support. And one of the best forms of therapy comes in the form of a brand new tailored suit, complete with waistcoat. Instead of the ready-made 'one-size-fits-all' demob version which came into being after World War Two, Walter would have paid for the bespoke suit out of a small allowance towards civilian clothes from the army, topped up by the earnings Emma had kept for him. Not just a suit, it feels like an acknowledgement of his return, and an acceptance of his place in peacetime Britain.

He must have been very proud of it to have kept the receipt from the tailor: 'Grey mixed Cheviot Lounge Suit sold to Walter Barley Esq by Forbes & Son, Hampstead, June 21, 1919, seven guineas.' There is an elegant Edwardian fit and flare to the jacket. The trousers have turnups and are tapered, in the style still prevalent after World War One. They make him look taller! Vi says he looks like the Prince of Wales.

She helps him into the jacket. He tucks his portfolio under his arm and steps out into the world. This enthusiastic, neatly-dressed young man with his jaunty air makes a good impression - his drawings are not bad either. Much to his delight he begins to receive some worthwhile commissions.

'Isn't it grand to get back, eh?' Rex Smith writes from Tunbridge Wells to his old army chum. Walter isn't quite so sure. Rex is bound to look at the world through rose-coloured spectacles - he has few family responsibilities, a permanent job in accountancy, and a steady girlfriend whom he's marrying in June.

The letter continues: 'The first thing I want settled is to know if you can be my best man; I want you for that far from enviable job above all others I know, especially as my brother and Florrie's brother are still out in Meso & India. The wedding will be only a quiet affair & as you have had such a wide experience of weddings, you will be a great help to me.'

Rex had made a good choice, not only because of Walter's wide experience of weddings. Although the two young men were as different as chalk from cheese -

Walter brimming with ideas, questioning everything and never happier than when he was in front of an audience, while Rex was quiet, methodical and unassuming – they complemented one another. During their sojourn in Mesopotamia they had discovered they shared many of the same ideals about life, love and war.

Now Walter has a focus outside his own preoccupations. Inspiration for his speech as best man comes into his head even before he finishes reading Rex's letter. He'll say something special about his old friend's strength of character, then put in a joke or two. Perhaps comment on his tidiness in the tent in Mesopotamia and reassure Florrie that Rex did not snore. Or would that bring a blush to her cheeks?

The quiet June wedding in Kent is very different from Susie's nuptials so graphically described by his precocious niece Doris. 'Oh Uncle Wallie, you should have been there!' She prattles on while Walter continues with his drawing.

Doris was a child of the post-war revolution in women's fashions. The boned bodices of pre-war years had no place in the lives of nurses at the battle-front or the girls who'd been working on the land or riding their bicycles to jobs in munitions factories. Skirts, Walter noticed, had risen to unprecedented heights during his absence and it was not unusual for a playful breeze to reveal a plump, rounded knee. To his pleasure and embarrassment, his appraising glance was often returned by a cheeky smile.

Time passes. Walter works far into the night on whatever is asked of him: posters, ideas for advertisements, finished artwork and endless, eye-straining lettering. He still finds plenty of time for a busy social life, playing tennis with Jim and Dorrie, whist with Ruby and having tea with sister Mabs. He sees Ethel and her family off to Australia and goes to the christening of Joe's second baby daughter. He misses Mr Hankinson's presence at Church where he sometimes does a prayer reading – the dapper little clergyman is on a mission in Hungary – goes for long walks in Hampstead and Chelsea and for rambles around the countryside. The gardens of Kenwood House, recently opened to the public, provide a welcome local retreat and a chance to contemplate the meaning of life, without coming to any definite conclusion.

But what is an attractive young man of twenty-four doing for so long without a girlfriend? Walter seems resigned to a bachelor's existence until his first diary since 1917 suggests otherwise.

Tuesday, 11th January 1921

Nita's birthday. It is a brilliant sunlit morning & I cycled on to the parliament hill before biz. to enjoy the air, I have not done this for such a long time.

Who is Nita? Perhaps Walter had met her at a concert or an art studio. Perhaps, on a whim, she had dropped her handkerchief in his path. Whatever the circumstances, their relationship seems well established by the time she makes an appearance.

Every week, an encouraging thought from Charles Letts, the diary's paternalistic publisher, brings Walter's thoughts back to business:

Saturday, 15th January 1921

'Better rise above your job than assume that your job is beneath you.'

Walter bears this in mind.

Friday, 4th March 1921

Muller Blatchleys. Interview with Mr Hughes. Small Chilprufe drawing to do. Whist drive with Ruby at Mrs Richardson's.

Monday, 7th March 1921

Interview with Mr Hughes re appointment. Take Chilprufe layout. He seems satisfied but requires me to call on him on Wednesday.

Tuesday, 8th March 1921

Exhibition card for Dunhill Sykes to be delivered on Thursday at 2.00pm. Worked until 12.30am.

And on Wednesday Hector Hughes, boss of Muller Blatchley studios, duly offers him a job, starting in ten days' time.

Next day, his finished Exhibition Card carefully wrapped and tucked under his arm, an elated Walter makes his way to the offices of Dunhill Sykes, not far from the prestigious clubs in Pall Mall and St James's. Dunhill's produced pipes, Sykes sent tobacco and a member of the family from America. Walter is now part of this newly flourishing business life in the West End of London. He admires the bright displays in the windows of Harry Selfridge's Oxford Street Store and catches the scent of Chanel No 5, surely the newest, most exclusive, expensive perfume in the world, wafting from behind shell-like ears and ostrich-feather collars as he strolls down Bond Street to make his delivery.

Thursday, 10th March 1921

Delivered Exhibition Card to Dunhill Sykes 1.45. Mr Sykes seemed quite pleased with the work, especially as I got it through to him on time.

Monday, 21st March 1921

Start at Muller & Blatchley.

This is a step in the right direction.

St George's Day, Saturday, 23rd April 1921

The day we dedicate to the man who, for the Christians, was imprisoned by the Roman Emperor and died a martyr's death.

Tottenham Cup Final. King attends.

And what of Nita? Four months after her birthday she makes another enigmatic appearance in Walter's diary. His writing is hard to decipher and his tone is anguished:

Thursday, 12th May 1921

Walk with Nita through St James's Park to Victoria. Dance at R.C.A. put off. Walk over Wimbledon Common. Talk, and an admission. What is for the best? I will write.

Thursday, 26th May 1921

Met Nita. Dinner at Cheshire Cheese.

The famous Fleet Street pub was the haunt of actors and writers. Charlie Chaplin was spotted there in 1921, enjoying his cheese on toast, but Walter and Nita were more likely to have been intrigued by another of the pub's renowned characters: Polly the parrot, the centre of attraction after a recent, well-publicised escape through an open window.

> Polly had been given up for lost, when a man walking along Farringdon Avenue was invited to 'Give me a kiss darling.' 'Certainly not!' he replied. The disembodied voice then demanded, 'Pudding and two veg, and hurry up!'

It was not a lady of the night with a croaky throat, but Polly, who was caught and with much rejoicing brought back to the pub.

That evening, Walter has other things on his mind than the smart-talking parrot; he is concerned about his relationship with Nita.

Having walked her to her train, he writes of his doubts in his diary: *'Is this to be au revoir?* The next sentence, almost illegible, ends on a hopeful note. *'Nita will write. An invitation.'*

There is no letter, no invitation. Then comes more good news about his career and a pivotal reunion with Nita.

Wednesday, 18th June 1921

Rise from Muller Blatchley, also expression of satisfaction.

Wednesday, 31st August 1921

Met Nita Charing X at Corner House. Walk to station and then from Putney. Nita is going to Eastbourne to teach art & gym at a Girl's college.

They are together for the last time a week later. Walter's writing is almost illegible:

Tuesday, 6th September 1921

Beggars Opera with Nita. Then on platform I am in doubt, & Nita? I walk home and feel that what I have said [illegible]*...I look back* [illegible]*...*

Wednesday, 7th September 1921

Oh I feel that I have done wrong, great wrong to her and perhaps to myself. But what have I done to you my dear, dear friend. Oh Nita, Nita, I will be true and if in trying to do right I fail [illegible]*...*

The homily in this week's diary is sadly appropriate for Walter's circumstances: *'Every twenty-four hours people are older and wiser and more discriminating – life is constantly evolving change.'*

And so Nita's train takes her away to a new life, and Walter trudges gloomily home through deserted streets.

The house at 27 Archibald Road is in darkness. He opens the front door as quietly as he can, but young Alistair starts crying. He can see a light under the door and hear snatches of the Gaelic lullaby Betty sings as she tries to soothe him back to sleep. Walter climbs the stairs to bed.

He loves his little nephew and wonders whether he will have children of his own, one day. He sighs. He has his parents to look after and in spite of his recent pay rise it will take years for him to earn enough money to afford a wife, a home and to start a family. In his imagination he has tried to picture his future wife sitting beside him by the fireside, their child chuckling on her knee. For a few moments of elation, he had thought it might be Nita.

He looks out at the starlit night and thinks back to a time when life was less complicated, when one slept under canvas and lived for the moment.

Only a page of the following undated letter to Rex Smith survives. It was sent to him in the late 1960s by Florrie, after Rex's death.

Meso had been hell for many British troops, but for Walter it is never to lose its association with the Garden of Eden.

'My dear Rex,

'Just a line before I turn in. It is 10.00pm & times were when at this hour we would be finishing up the remainder of the "hot char" & preparing to go each to his own "araby" bed in a corner of one of those EP tents we knew at Hambis & Baqubah.

'The fresh mornings & evenings we are just experiencing bring to mind those glorious frosty winter days & nights in the wilderness when the air came like a refreshing wine after the summer heat & kindled a new spirit in a man. I can imagine hearing you about your morning ablutions & the click of your safety razor when the early morning sunlight had climbed over the canal bank that sheltered us, & we were making ready for a walk over to the canal heads, or the suspension bridge that swung over the Khurrasion Canal, a walk that meant wet boots in the dew soaked grass...'

Years later, when Walter has married and made his way in the world, he still holds these moments of tranquillity in his heart.

Epilogue

When some doors close, others open

1922 My mother met Walter at the Muller Blatchley studio, where she was an aspiring young illustrator. He was captivated by her shy charm, and she fell in love with him instantly - he was quite unlike any of the young men she had met at home in Gloucestershire. His enthusiasm and excitement about his work was infectious. She admired his ideas for posters and drawings, especially those in the latest style - known as Art Deco since the 1919 'Exposition Internationale des Arts Décoratifs et Industriels Modernes' in Paris. Bold shapes and muted colours were typical of Walter's designs for shipping lines and his advertisements for Chilprufe woollen underwear for children. Some of them passed into the archives of advertising history. Talented though she was, Eileen's delicate drawings were never commercially successful. Her father did not approve of Walter and sent her to stay with cousins in Queensland, supposedly hoping she'd marry a rich sheep farmer. Walter intended to follow her but failed his medical test. Having worked so hard to make his way with his career, he may not, at heart, been very enthusiastic about leaving England and his family. And he'd had enough of hot weather.

1923 Percy died at the age of 38. The Barleys rallied round the family, Walter spending a lot of time with Alastair as he grew from a toddler into a demanding little boy who did not take kindly to Walter's new girlfriend. Eileen remembered him throwing lumps of mud at her when she first visited 27 Archibald Road, but they became friends when he grew up. His mother Betty, the gentle girl from the Highlands, found it hard to cope with two energetic children and life with the rumbustious Barley family. After breaking her leg one winter she signed herself into a nursing home where she spent the rest of her long life. Percy was a Mason and the local lodge appointed a guardian to look after the children's affairs. They both gained scholarships to Masonic boarding schools and did well.

1926 James made Percy's daughter Christine a dolls' house. At 74, he retained his woodworking skills and in later life he was popular with his grandchildren, who called him 'Pom Pom'.

1927 Walter, Emma, James and Vi moved to 9, Argyle Road, a comfortable semi in Finchley. They named it 'Eothen' after Alexander William Kinglake's popular account of his travels in the Middle East.

Walter was under considerable stress, working too hard, worrying about Emma and James and arguing with his sister Vi. He took up faith-healing and joined a peace movement. His diary shows his concern about his relationships with other people:

Friday, 17th August, 1928

I speak to Vi – heated words & I brutally box her ears. The regret of it all.

Saturday, 18th August, 1928

The grave relics of Ur of the Caldeans, 3,500BC. The chance passing of the boy in buttons that once figured in a vision – of fear.

He left his comfortable job at Muller Blatchley for a better-paid position with more responsibility, but it was not a success. He went back to free-lance work, taking commissions where he could, including painting scenery for a Soho nightclub. His work improved in its scope and professionalism when he went to evening classes at St Martin's School of Art.

1934 Emma died at the age of 82. Fred Hankinson, home from his mission in Hungary, presided at her funeral. Even after his Oxford education, he retained traces of his dry Altrincham accent. His voice had none of the theatricality of some preachers of the time, but the cadence of his language and the sincerity of his tone had many of his large congregation in tears.

'...At last the call has come to her, the Heavenly Summons has been received and

God has taken her into the Spirit Land. When she was even in failing health, bearing her illness with bravery and endurance, she still loved life and all it brought her of Love and Friendship...'

'...She was blessed, as she oftentimes said, by having so many of her children and grandchildren around her, and with what a happy pride she read out the letters received from her loved ones abroad. In her active days she was a real wonder, owing to her energy, her power of administering her home and caring for her large family...'

Eileen was back in England, disillusioned with sheep farmers, and had a calming influence on Walter, whose career took off when he joined the firm of Thomas Dixon, owner of an up-coming advertising agency in Wimbledon. Eileen's father then packed her off to Germany to learn the language. She was an apt pupil and enjoyed the atmosphere of 1930s Berlin, becoming a fan of the Bauhaus movement, but was alarmed by Hitler's increasing popularity, especially as she believed the family she was staying with was Jewish. And she missed Walter. She returned to England and got pregnant. Walter did the honourable thing.

1937 Walter and Eileen married and moved to a small flat in Wembley Park where I was born an almost respectable six months later. I flourished on Cow & Gate powdered milk. Walter was a loving, indulgent father. Eileen's father married his housekeeper to whom he left all his money. Fortuitously a legacy from a benevolent aunt enabled Eileen to commission her architect brother-in-law to build a house at Moor Lane, Rickmansworth, on what was then part of a long field on the edge of Moor Park Golf Course. They lived there, more or less happily, ever after. Walter kept bees, grew celery and apple trees and the couple made hand-hooked rugs together in the evenings, to Eileen's Bauhaus-based designs.

1938 I was born on a cold, January evening.

1939 Walter wrote a long letter to me on my 1st birthday. I only discovered it after his death.

13 Lawns Court
The Avenue
Barn Hill
Wembley
Middx.

'Dear Helen Ruth,

'Today your mother & I greet you on your first birthday. What a year it has been for you. How busy you have been ever since you began to take notice of things & shapes. How we welcomed your first quiet smile – which soon grew into a chuckle & then a merry laugh, & how busy you have made your mother, every day taken up with our feedings & washings & makings of garments. You can now say one word clearly, 'pretty'. You say many other sounds not so intelligible to us but full of meaning to you. You have also eight teeth, well-spaced, four at the top and four below. (At 3 months you had 3 teeth – the first of which even puzzled the doctor who, concerned with your tummy, did not think so young a baby could be cutting teeth. But you put him and us at rest when we found that was the cause.)

'…Today we have bought a cup and spoon for you, symbols of your attaining a new experience – of being able to eat solid food – & we are pleased to think that soon you will not need a bottle but will sit up with us to your meals at our table. Your mother is making a cake for you – sponge – with almond icing with walnuts & cherries on top. This year you will be able to partake of the sponge only...

'...Your mother says you love the sunshine – I hope you will always love the sun & all the beautiful things of the earth because they call forth beautiful thoughts which are the most priceless things in all the world.

'Many happy returns to our little daughter

'Walter & Eileen.'

1941 James dies, aged 88. Mr Hankinson's eulogy is the epitome of tact:

'...There were many ups and downs, difficulties and struggles in his long life and, at times, there was shadow and suffering, but it is really a matter of rejoicing that in his latter years there came a calm and quietness, and a gladness in his life, and we can truly say, his end was peace, we all know his genuine love for good music and though sometimes there were discords in his life, the spirit of his musical nature brought in the end harmony and song...

'...We recall him in his business days, his good and thorough workmanship and his thoughtfulness in carrying out the task in hand to the very best of his abilities. In this work he comforted many when Death entered some home and he did his undertaking in a quiet and refined manner, and I, as a minister, can bear witness to this. And now the workman lays down his tools that others may carry out that service for him. It seemed as if God had given him a long life in order to round off his life at last into a calm...'

1942 My brother was born on June 13th, at home in Moor Lane, located directly under the flight path for blitz raids by the Luftwaffe on targets north of London. He was christened by Mr Hankinson, then aged 67, who sprinkled cold water on his head from a pink porridge bowl. You had to use what was to hand in wartime. The startled baby burst into tears. Walter tenderly gathered him into his arms and carried him into the sunlit garden. High above them an RAF Spitfire doodled a lazy vapour trail across the blue sky before tipping its wings, picking up speed and resuming its flight back to base.

Guadalmina, 2017

Six Poems and an Anecdote

This small selection includes some of Walter's favourite verses from his childhood, as well as poems that describe with bitter irony the conditions and effects of the war in Mesopotamia. There is also a piece of entertainingly bad doggerel.

The Better Land
Felicia Hemans, 1793-1835

I hear thee speak of the better land,
Thou call'st its children a happy band
Mother! oh, where is that radiant shore?
Shall we not seek it, and weep no more?
Is it where the flower of the orange blows,
And the fire-flies glance thro' the myrtle boughs?
– Not there, not there, my child!

Is it where the feathery palm-trees rise,
And the date grows ripe under sunny skies?
Or midst the green islands of glittering seas,
Where fragrant forests perfume the breeze,

And strange bright birds on their starry wings
Bear the rich hues of all glorious things?
– Not there, not there, my child!

Is it far away, in some region old,
Where the rivers flow o'er sands of gold,
Where the burning rays of the ruby shine,
And the diamond lights up the secret mine,
And the pearl gleams forth from the coral strand?
Is it there, sweet mother! that better land?"
– Not there, not there, my child!

Eye hath not seen it, my gentle boy!
Ear hath not heard its songs of joy!
Dreams cannot picture a world so fair –
Sorrow and death may not enter there:
Time doth not breathe on its fadeless bloom
For beyond the clouds and beyond the tomb,
– It is there, it is there, my child!

Casablanca
Felicia Hemans, 1793-1835

The boy stood on the burning deck
Whence all but he had fled;
The flame that lit the battle's wreck
Shone round him o'er the dead.
Yet beautiful and bright he stood,
As born to rule the storm;

A creature of heroic blood,
A proud, though child-like form.
The flames rolled on – he would not go
Without his Father's word;
That father, faint in death below,
His voice no longer heard.
He called aloud – 'Say, Father, say
If yet my task is done?'
He knew not that the chieftain lay
Unconscious of his son.
'Speak, father!' once again he cried,
'If I may yet be gone!'
And but the booming shots replied,
And fast the flames rolled on.
Upon his brow he felt their breath,
And in his waving hair,
And looked from that lone post of death
In still yet brave despair.
And shouted but once more aloud,
'My father! must I stay?'
While o'er him fast, through sail and shroud,
The wreathing fires made way.
They wrapt the ship in splendour wild,
They caught the flag on high,
And streamed above the gallant child,
Like banners in the sky.
There came a burst of thunder sound –
The boy – oh! where was he?
Ask of the winds that far around
With fragments strewed the sea! –
With mast, and helm, and pennon fair,
That well had borne their part –
But the noblest thing which perished there
Was that young faithful heart.

This poem was much parodied at the time. Walter might have enjoyed these examples:

> The boy stood on the burning deck.
> When he could stand no more
> He found a cake of ivory soap
> And washed himself ashore.
>
> The boy stood on the burning deck,
> His feet were full of blisters.
> His socks had burned right off his feet.
> He had to wear his sister's.
>
> The boy stood on the burning deck,
> It simply wasn't cricket.
> A canon ball went up his leg
> And stumped his middle wicket.

Vespers
T. E. Brown, 1830-1897, published 1900

> O blackbird, what a boy you are!
> How you do go it!
> Blowing your bugle to that one sweet star...
> How you do blow it!
> And does she hear you, blackbird boy, so far?
> Or is it wasted breath?
> 'Good Lord! she is so bright
> To-night!'
> The blackbird saith.

Abbottabad
Sir James Abbott, 1805-1896

I remember the day when I first came here
And smelt the sweet Abbottabad air,

The trees and ground covered with snow
Gave us indeed a brilliant show.

To me the place seemed like a dream
And far ran a lonesome stream.

The wind hissed as if welcoming us
The pine swayed creating a lot of fuss

And the tiny cuckoo sang it away,
A song very melodious and gay.

I adored the place from the first sight
And was happy that my coming here was right

And eight good years here passed very soon
And we leave you perhaps on a sunny noon.

Oh Abbottabad we are leaving you now
To your natural beauty do I bow.

Perhaps your wind's sound will never reach
my ears.
My gift for you is a few sad tears.

I bid you farewell with a heavy heart
Never from my mind will your memories thwart.

Sir James was an intrepid soldier and an able, if controversial, Deputy Commissioner. Poetry was evidently not his strong point.

Mesopotamia
Rudyard Kipling, 1805-1936

They shall not return to us, the resolute, the young,
The eager and whole-hearted whom we gave:
But the men who left them thriftily to die in their own dung,
Shall they come with years and honour to the grave?

They shall not return to us; the strong men coldly slain
In sight of help denied from day to day:
But the men who edged their agonies and chid them in their pain,
Are they too strong and wise to put away?

Our dead shall not return to us while Day and Night divide –
Never while the bars of sunset hold.
But the idle-minded overlings who quibbled while they died,
Shall they thrust for high employments as of old?

Shall we only threaten and be angry for an hour:
When the storm is ended shall we find
How softly but how swiftly they have sidled back to power

By the favour and contrivance of their kind?

Even while they soothe us, while they promise large amends,
Even while they make a show of fear,
Do they call upon their debtors, and take counsel with their friends,
To conform and re-establish each career?

Their lives cannot repay us – their death could not undo –
The shame that they have laid upon our race.
But the slothfulness that wasted and the arrogance that slew,
Shall we leave it unabated in its place?

A Mesopotamian Alphabet
Anonymous

A was an apple that grew, so they say
In the Garden of Eden down Kurna way,
Till Eve came along and ate it one day
And got thrown out of Mesopotamia.

B Is the biscuit that's made down in Delhi
It breaks your teeth and bruises your belli,
And grinds your intestines into jelli,
In the land of Mesopotamia.

C is the poor old Indian Corps
Which went to France and fought in the War,
Now it gathers the corp's and fights no more,
In the land of Mesopotamia.

D is the digging we've all of us done,
Since first we started to fight the Hun,
And by now we've shifted ten thousand ton
Of Mutti, in Mesopotamia.

E was in energy shown by the staff,
Before the much advertised Hanna strafe,
Yet the net results was the Turks had a laugh
At our staff in Mesopotamia.

F stands for Fritz, who flies in the sky,
To bring the Brute down we've had many a try,
Yet the shells that we shoot at him all pass him by,
And fall on Mesopotamia.

G is the grazing we do all the day,
We fervently hope that some day we may
Get issued again with a ration of hay,
Although we're in Mesopotamia.

H are the Harems – which, it appears,
Have flourished in Baghdad for hundreds of years.
We propose to annex all the Destitute Dears
When their husbands die in Mesopotamia.

I is the Indian Government... but... but
On this subject I'm told I must keep my mouth shut,
For it's all due to them that we didn't reach Kut-El-Amara, in Mesopotamia.

J is the jam with the German label that lies, lies, lies,
And states that in 'Berlin' it won the first prize,
But out here we use it for catching the flies,
That swarm in Mesopotamia.

K are the kisses from lips sweet and fair
Waiting for us around Leicester Square
When we wend our way home after wasting a year
Or two in Mesopotamia.

L is the loot which we hope we shall seize,
Wives, and wine, and bags of rupees,
When the Mayor of Baghdad hands over his keys
To the British in Mesopotamia.

M is the local mosquito whose bite
Keeps us awake all the hours of the night
And makes all our faces a horrible sight,
In this land of Mesopotamia.

N is the Navy that's tied to the shore
They've lashings of beer and stores galore.
Oh I wish I'd joined up in the Navy before
I came to Mesopotamia.

O are the Orders we get from the Corps.
'Thank God' by now we are perfectly sure
If issued at three, they'll be cancelled at four,
By the Muddlers in Mesopotamia.

P are the Postal Officials who fail
To deliver each week more than half of our mail;
If they had their deserts they would all be in jail –
Instead of Mesopotamia.

Q's the quinine, which we take every day
To keep the Malarial fever away,
Which we're bound to get sooner or later they say
If we stop in Mesopotamia.

R are the rations they give us to eat –
For breakfast there's biscuits; for dinner there's meat,

And if we've been good we get jam for a treat
With our tea in Mesopotamia.

S & **T** are supposed to supply, 'God forbid,'
The Army with food – we all hope when they die
They all go to a place as hot as H--- and as dry
As this horrible Mesopotamia.

U is the lake called Um-El-Brahm,
Which guards our flank from all possible harm,
And waters General Garange's barley farm,
In the middle of Mesopotamia.

V was the victory won at Dujailah,
I heard it first from a friend who's a sailor,
Who read it in Reuter's on board his Mahela,
On the Tigris in Mesopotamia.

W stands for wonder and pain,
With which we regard the infirm and insane
Indian Generals who fund the campaign
We are waging in Mesopotamia.

X are the Extras the Corps say we get
But so far there isn't a unit I've met
That has drawn a single one of them yet,
Since they landed in Mesopotamia.

Y is the yearning we feel every day
For a passage to Basra, and then to Bombay –
If we get there we'll see that we stay well away
From this wilderness, Mesopotamia.

Z I tried very hard, and finally hit
On a verse which a 'Z' might easily fit,
But the Censor deleted every bit,
Save the last words 'for God's sake – Mesopotamia.'

Lord Hardinge of Penhurst and the Smoking Chimney

Field Marshall Sir Henry Hardinge lived in a Victorian pile on the Penshurst estate in Kent when he was raised to the peerage and became Viceroy of India. His neighbour Lord de L'Isle and Dudley, whose family seat had been Penshurst Place for generations, regarded him as rather an upstart, but courteously invited him to tea under the ancestral cedar trees. Hardinge looked up at the imposing old house. 'Upon my word,' he remarked, 'your chimney is smoking!' Lord de L'Isle arched an eyebrow and replied, 'When your family has lived here as long as mine, Hardinge, your own chimney will smoke.'